THIS ASSIGNMENT IS SO GAY

lgbtiq poets on the art of teaching

edited by
MEGAN VOLPERT

SiblingRivalryPress

ALEXANDER, ARKANSAS
WWW.SIBLINGRIVALRYPRESS.COM

This assignment is so gay: LGBTIQ Poets on the Art of Teaching
Copyright © 2013 by Megan Volpert

Cover Design by Mona Z. Kraculdy

Sibling Rivalry Press, LLC
13913 Magnolia Glen Drive
Alexander, AR 72002

www.siblingrivalrypress.com
info@siblingrivalrypress.com

ISBN: 978-1-937420-42-0

Library of Congress Control Number: 2013935224

First Sibling Rivalry Press Edition, August 2013

The translation of the fragment of Sappho quoted by Pablo Miguel Martínez in "Fragment 16" is by Anne Carson, as published in If Not, Winter: Fragments of Sappho (Knopf, 2002).

CONTENTS

INTRODUCTON

Of course "it gets better." Dan Savage's idea was so simple that it could not fail to plant seeds of strength in the hearts of young people across the world. But for so many children, graduation is a distant light at the end of a very terrifying tunnel. Perhaps the real world will welcome them with open arms. Perhaps they will finally be free to be themselves—if only they can hang on long enough. The promise of those three little words often will not suffice.

That's why I returned to the scene of the crime. Educational institutions are the breeding ground for ideas, delivery systems for a knowledge of self-worth that can speak truth to powerful bullies long before it's time to march off in a cap and gown. There is definite room for the so-called gay agenda in schools, and that's why I became a teacher: the celebration of diversity, the promotion of acceptance, the protection of equality.

The very existence of an LGBTIQ-identified teacher in the classroom is still an act of revolution. We are life rafts in the bloodbath of adolescent identity politics. We are role models to all and unicorns to many. We preserve a space for a fledging feeling in the heart of a child that many narrow-minded grown people would prefer to see stomped out, even if they have to extinguish the whole child with it.

That's why they keep trying to get rid of us. In 1978, The Briggs Initiative attempted to ban homosexuals from teaching in California's public schools. This was well after the Civil Rights Movement, but if it still feels like ancient history, we can look at the steady stream of faculty leaving Georgia's Shorter University last year after being asked to sign a "personal lifestyle statement" that condemned homosexuality. Examples of this injustice are abundant and though there is no federal protection for employment discrimination based on sexual orientation, the problem of protecting queer jobs in my own backyard almost seems droll compared to the problem of protecting queer lives in the broader international scene.

So it's kind of amazing that all the teachers you will find in these pages have the courage to announce themselves as LGBTIQ to the world—a world that includes many people who dislike and fear them, and who have influence upon their careers. I myself have sweated it out in the principal's

15

office to defend against much less grievously queer offenses than the publication of this anthology. I wonder if there is any chance my school's library will be permitted to loan out this book sometime before I retire.

There is so much more work to do. Much of that work is described within these pages. Not all the poems directly address queer matters, of course, because teachers have many things to do in a day besides pondering their own sexual orientation. What echoes consistently across these pages instead is a special kind of attention to the ethics of caring. Yeah, the students need saving and quickly—and they're not the only ones.

The world gets better because teachers are making it better. All kinds of teachers, including those identifying as LGBTIQ, are needed in the service of this mission. Legislators, administrators, parents, students and other teachers must come to understand that the future depends on it. This anthology is intended to aid in that discovery.

Yours,

Megan Volpert

THIS
ASSIGNMENT
IS
SO
GAY

GERARD WOZEK

AN OPEN LETTER TO MY STUDENTS

What I want you to know is that these lives
matter.

When we read *Leaves of Grass* and one of you
shrugs, who cares that Walt Whitman loved men?
Or questions, so what if Tennessee Williams
wrote a gay subtext for the character of Tom
in *The Glass Menagerie?* Or declares that there
is no significance whatsoever in the homosexual
affectations with Oscar Wilde's *Dorian Gray*,
or downplays the erotic encounter between
Shug and Celie in Alice Walker's *The Color Purple*,
or laughs off the bond between Sebastian
and Charles in Evelyn Waugh's *Brideshead Revisited*.

Take note. These acts of love hold significance.

Throughout history, before and after labels,
there was always an impulse toward making fire:
woman to woman, man to man, one being to another
being. Mark it down. We burned for one another.
We risked everything. Sometimes we fought or tried
to deny the passion seeking confirmation. Despite
the blight of cultural trends that erase or ignore
or dismiss our heritage, we persist.
Writing into the night. Offering the whole story.

So this quarter in the classroom we will examine
and explicate and attempt to come to terms with
the visionary transgendering in Virginia Woolf's
character Orlando, the spark between David and Joey
in James Baldwin's *Giovanni's Room*, the love poems
in Adrienne Rich's *Dream of a Common Language*.

If we can enter the life of but one of these characters
with compassionate surrendering. If we can come to
see one protagonist's desire to love freely in a world
dead set against their truth flowering open. Then we
can allow that flame that exists in the text to leap
off the page and set up a bonfire in our own heart.
And what a sweet, unforgettable burn it can be.

GREGORY WOODS

PLATONIC DIALOGUE

I speak you listen
you speak I listen
I ask you questions
you give me answers
you ask me questions
I give you answers
I outline a fact
you repeat the fact
I outline a theory
you question the theory
I tell a laboured joke
you forgive with laughter
you tell a rude joke
I pretend to be shocked
I write on the board
you write in your notebook
I frown you frown
you smile I smile
you frown I frown
I smile you smile
you chew your pencil
you scratch your temple
I teach you learn
you learn I learn
I fall silent
you fall silent
I get bored with you
you get bored with me
I stifle a yawn
you stifle a laugh
I make you work
you make me work

you read what I've written
I read what you've written
I teach from experience
you learn by experience
I recite what I've memorized
you memorize what I recite
I want you to say it again
you want me to say it again
you learn by heart
I teach by heart
my voice in your ear
my words on your lips
I stay here you go there
your life is there
here your chewed pencil

NICHOLAS WONG

SUICIDE MISSION

Dear Americans, my mouth fails to thaw
your grief frozen by collision. Limbs of time callused,

the world stood still, survivors shrouded by
dust delivered by Federal Express—eternal

inferno. There's no such thing called
survival, tragedies always pending, language

second-hand in outlining the loan of pain.
No matter what I say, I'll be accused of skindeep

sympathy. Today, a student with yellow skin
found *United 93* boring. I didn't blame him, his corneas

over-drugged by digital images. Even deaths, these
days, have to be diabolically 3D.

I rescued the intellect of my class with the last
bits of the film—jerky camerawork, tilted shots,

overlapping diegetic dialogues, all cause
claustrophobia. Subtitle said engine whining, many

hands on the steering wheel, one antagonistic
to others. Blackout. The student shook

his head, frame of reference regained. He asked,
Did they die? I said it's a gap he had to

fill up himself. He left, leaving the evaluation
blank, the way absence revenges. I put the

DVD back to its case, the cover a mosaic of
American faces, all burning like tangerines.

CYRIL WONG

CREATIVE WRITING

What rhymes with gay: fray, say,
a sun-filled day . . .
Okay,
I tell our adopted son,
peering up from his homework
at both his fathers.

Use the words in a poem:
Stars were bright and gay
at the end of the day
in the beginning of May . . .

Stopping short of instructions
bitter on the tongue,
buried meanings we yearn to transform
through lessons of courage
and sweet defiance

too foreign for our child to take
or so we thought.

But you are gay too, right?
Can I write about my daddies?
So what do I say?

Gay as in happy
or angry; rainbows and unicorns
or a bloodied war-cry—
I keep my thoughts to myself.

Say what you know
to be true, my partner instructs him.

24

The boy gazes out the window

for a moment, before returning
to his notebook, his pen
moving with a newfound purpose

that chills us, even as our hearts
could never be more full.

RIVER WOLTON

THERE'S ALWAYS ONE,

they'll warn you of him
and his name will toll
at ever frequent intervals.
    He'll jump in
blunt, will barely write, will smirk and kick.
You'll force aside the urge to slap;
no one will want to work with him.
    And yet
he'll rap to sonnets, break-dance
to limericks, say that cushions are 'like toast,'
warm to the applause and want to play each part.
    With luck
you'll keep him from the corridor, the Head,
and (despite yourself, despite the girls
bowed over their desks) you'll whisper
      praise.
Years on, he'll be the only face you can recall,
and you'll cross your fingers
that he didn't make the news.

SCOTT WIGGERMAN

ADVOCATE

They come to me like penitents,
past the pink triangle on my door:

plodding gaits, jittery eyes,
voices that seldom rise above whispers.

They confess: *I think I might be gay.*
They want absolution, not realizing

the canyon between secrets and sins.
I'm often the first adult they've

spoken these words to, the only teacher
they've known who's out.

I listen. I don't have to coax.
The pressure of dammed-up silence

unleashes floods of words,
the long breath after time underwater.

I give them my blessing: *It's okay.*
And add: *Don't ever apologize.*

SCOTT WIGGERMAN

DAY OF SILENCE

for the Gay-Straight Alliances

You think you know them, these students
who can't remember to bring a pencil to class
but somehow manage to find pink duct tape.

You told them their silence would be enough,
but they insisted on covering their mouths
with bright rectangles of sticky shocking pink.

The words of taped mouths can't be suppressed.
With eyes on fire, these gay and straight students
blaze down the halls, their message incinerating:
What are you going to do to end the silence?

SCOTT WIGGERMAN

TEACHING TOLERANCE

Without hesitation, the clip-ons went on,
each earring dangling a thumb-sized heart
encrusted in a thin coat of Chinese silver.

Then, the tiara: seven spikes of purple jewels
surrounding a central, sparkly red gem,
heart-shaped to match the earrings,

a pièce de résistance of hard plastic
that sent waves of *oohs* and *ahhs*—
laughter so hard the windows shook.

I was delighted with the Dollar Store gift—
we all were—as I paraded down rows of desks,
waving at my students as if I were on a float.

The teenagers all took turns being a queen—
gay, straight, Christian, Jew, white, black.
What did the manufacturers know, *ages 4-8?*

I turned fifty with my best working birthday ever.

MEGAN VOLPERT

HUNTER THOMPSON IS SUGAR-FREE

He calls at four to bark and mutter concerning black tongue, about which I know nothing except that I am awake. The cell battery increasingly beeps and finally dies, then the man is dead, just as I approach vision focus purpose readiness openness to the energy of greater something. In the classroom like it is still all good, my students want a clear definition of transcendentalism. I pull it together too slowly until they are freaked into wondering what will be on the test, except for the stoned kid in the corner who asks what Owl Farm is. The earth immediately resumes rotation because I am sharing airspace with this kid.

MEGAN VOLPERT

THIS IS BROWN BEAR SOUP

That's what my little brother said at age three, when our grandpa asked him why he was battering an empty bowl with a wooden spoon. My brother and I grew up in the same house, but I didn't know I didn't know him until I watched him huff a Sharpie to get high in rehab. He is wanted for felonies in two states, but he managed to get his GED first. I teach like I am on one of those cop shows where a hardcase joins the force to avenge the fact that his sister was abducted when they were kids. If only he'd been a little more vigilant and needling blame games like that.

MEGAN VOLPERT

YOU ARE SUSPENDED

When I was a kid, nobody I knew was out of the closet. Actually, I didn't know anybody who was in the closet either. There were rumors about an English teacher that made her my favorite, but then other rumors about why I was her favorite. Some people become the thing they try to escape, and others become the thing that saves them. Ducking and covering across the many barriers to my certification, I conjure before you the only openly queer faculty member in this public Southern high school, fully equipped to teach both English and tolerance. You are failing tolerance and that's why I wrote you up. You're welcome.

DANIEL NATHAN TERRY

A STUDENT SAYS SHE HATES NATURE POETRY

and is glad that Bishop and Frost are dead
along with their rainbows, birds and golden leaves.

She wants the poetry of pavement,
bars, dirty sheets and drugs. Real life,

she insists, has nothing to do with birds,
forest paths or things that grow. Never mind

her pavement's made of earth, her bar
of wood, her dirty sheets made of cotton

and the skin of the night. Never mind
that her drugs were distilled from green leaves

that were, for a moment, golden
on a mountainside that faced

the Columbian sun. Never mind that
when she takes that gold into her blood

she becomes its sister and this reunion fills her
with something close to birdsong.

DANIEL NATHAN TERRY

THE MEETING

All the day long, there was nothing of note.
Between classes, I sat and waited on the bench
beside the retention pond on campus.

Three duck decoys, placed there
months ago by Environmental Studies
to attract real ducks, listed in the wind—moving,

but fooling no one. I imagined how beautiful
the arrival of living mallards or teal would be—
whir of wings, the wake and ripples

they would make on the surface. But students passed
without looking. There was nothing for any of us
on the dark water. Then, just as I considered

looking for a new spot, a blue heron stretched
his slender neck from the tall, dry reeds
that lined the bank, only feet away from where I sat.

With one silver eye, wide as the winter moon,
he looked at me, as if I were the one
who was unexpected.

YERMIYAHU AHRON TAUB

BIRDWATCHING WITHOUT BINOCULARS

I have not survived the culture war(s) unscathed.
Quite the contrary.
In fact, some say I have post-traumatic stress disorder.
Others counter such claims.
Apparently it's not like being pregnant. Hmm . . .
Why don't we work to uncover the trajectory of things, they propose,
how the blessing of night has come to elude you,
how you have catapulted supine onto this gangplank.

Years of finessing the same basic arguments to indifferent or
hostile ears have taken their toll, I respond.
Even back then, I wondered if I was changing minds, but I felt I had to
remain a combatant, that I could not leave the trenches, that there was
necessarily honor in the battle. Isn't that what the young did?
Perhaps I also felt that the powers of my argumentation were being
honed amidst the barrage returned at me, that in the dodging of volleys
I was somehow becoming limber and loose.

But the staccato of my step only led to new questions.
Despite my determination on various fronts—home, school, barricade—
whom had I reached, let alone taught? Would I ever know?
And where once I thought a truce had been declared,
I now understood otherwise. The rhetoric that once was has returned,
more virulent than ever. I see that this war has not
ended, that perhaps it may never. Is war inherently finite?
If it has no end, is it something other than war?

Enough of these pontifications, their eyes declaim even as they
listen politely. How does this make you *feel*? If the personal is political,
is the political not also personal? I retreat from their prodding and
lean into the pane, spotting sparrows in trees.
I once thought I could escape into their world, or at least into its scrutiny:

call, gray/brown, flight, streak. I too can detect and dissect. But the war (or whatever this is) will not release me, and so I turn away, aware now of blood dribbling on beige. This couch will have to be reupholstered.

YERMIYAHU AHRON TAUB

PIED PIPER ON HOLIDAY

After disembarking from the taxi, he locates the room advertised,
the words "discreet" and "private" the only clues given (or needed).
He scans the view of the courtyard, the one less cherished than that of
the village or the mountains: the fruit trees, the mosaics,
the fountain *gurgling*. Was that the word he wanted? He is pleased by
the iron bed with its rough blanket, the paint flaking off the walls,
the porcelain water pitcher and bowl, and the flowered border of
the white cloth crossing the night stand
that serves as the lone ornamentation in the room.

He is familiar with rooms such as this one, and, in fact, prefers them to his
own, with their studied refinement and curios briefly registered: Zagreb,
September 19–, Jarbah Island, ? Such is his manner at home: cautious
but eclectic. It is enough that he does such work by day, well not exactly,
since he often works into the night. Let us say it is enough that this is
his livelihood, to which he is devoted and well-regarded by the few who
know and care. At home, he permits himself some slack, or freedom,
shall we say further. And yet some continuity must be maintained.
He is amused by these pleasures, minor they may be.

He hears voices in reflection, not muffled exactly, but modulated,
and is glad for them, for the tautness of their contribution to
his time here. He remembers the anticipation of long ago, the sounds of
children entering the schoolyard. How he pooled his calm prior to
each lesson, how he drew the children in with his tales, savored the
transformation of their restlessness into rapture. What others would later
call seduction. When he considers the verb "to sack," he thinks
of sackcloth and how, yes, there is a kind of mourning that happens,
or ought to, in any case.

Not only for those children, whose names he whispers: P, M . . . But for
others like them who . . . For the children of the children who might have

reminded him of their parents. For the chalk dust, for the giggles, for the penmanship shedding tentativeness. Instead, he will catalog objects, to ensure their importance in the history of loveliness. He will hope that the children who might have been will come upon them. And he will remain glad for rooms such as this one, with their blankness, in these varied cities, where certain kinds of connections can be made, where certain kinds of comfort can be found.

GABRIEL SYLVIAN, TRANSLATOR
ORIGINAL POEM BY GI HYEONG-DO

SOUND BONES

Professor Gim published a new academic theory
that sounds also have bones.
Everyone laughed it off. A few scholars
thanked Gim for the humor and the moment's amusement.
Despite a strong warning from the university president.
the professor opened up a class for one semester.
Students, curious, registered for the course as a joke.
At every class meeting
for the entire term he was silent, manifesting a frightening
intractableness.
Unable to stand it any longer, students gave their personal points of view about
what a sound
bone is.
One student, Lee, said it was silence.
Another student, Park, saw it as hidden meaning.
Another said the concept wasn't important.
It was a methodological metaphor chosen for the purpose of enacting a critique
of all fixed
concepts.
The professor's view was too difficult to comprehend and soon silenced.
But regardless
from the next semester our ears
heard sounds much better than before.

MOLLY SUTTON KIEFER

NEIGHBORING

Every afternoon, I listen at the wall of our classrooms,
the wary-thin plaster between us, and I hear him call out,
"If today is Wednesday, then tomorrow *is* . . ." His emphasis
sporadic, as if his prompting will coax the wheelchair bound students
to cry out perfect answers, to suddenly know where they belong
in this Habitrail school, aware that the sun means spring
has finally come, the blue banishing winter for another
howmanymonths. I walk past windows and open
doors, and I see the slack mouths, the faces pressed
against building blocks and storyboards.
I could lean in and stand a moment,
listen with my ear pressed to the glass, hear whispers
in honeyed tones on how to properly ask
to attend to privy needs. I could even
step in, place the whole of my body in the center
of the room and peel the bark of oranges, to see if taste buds bloom.
Instead, I return to my classroom, a sanctuary before the bell.
I can hear screaming, the lone howl wheezing again and again
just before lunch, always as my own students are reading aloud
from their Shakespeare, learning how to scan a sonnet,
tentatively trying it out on their own.

MOLLY SUTTON KIEFER

STUDENT TEACHING

I heard the word, edge of my ear: "———!" I cannot
even write it to think it, cannot overturn my appled art.
He was angry, this boy with the too-big glasses, wanted
something he couldn't describe, his hands scissoring out
against his classmate in metaphor, grappling, and there I was,
crouched, my heart punched out. I'm tired—is it night?
I cannot see the windows; my pulse funnels in my ear.
I remember the word inked on my best friend's shirt-back
like a tattoo. Will it help to spell it? *Eff.* I want to tunnel
into this boy's throat and leave dynamite. I want to pull
his tongue, let it hang low. He's angry; I am too. *Eh?*
Redirect into a question, ask: "Why are you upset?" Ask:
"Is there a better way to say that?" Try: nonverbal
communication. My eyes flit to sharpened pencils.
Gee. Aw, shucks, can't you tell I'm one of them,
my allegiance to some rainbow'ed flag. I scurry
to find some authority, confess the racket to the program
director and am urged: "Oh what luck—he can learn
from someone who *knows*." Cower and all that shame:
this curt shirt worn inside out.

SOPHIA STARMACK

EARTH SCIENCE

Holding up his project Jonah announces,
"There are billions of tiny orgasms living in the soil."

He's serene, studious, with blond ringlets
and a hand-drawn diagram of bedrock and roots.
I'm torn, but in the end I just can't correct an 11 year old

Week after week Jonah's parents ask me, *Is our son gay?*
Has he mastered his times tables yet?

Ten times a day I fantasize about telling them the truth:
Your son, I will say, is a genius of depravity.
Right now he's facing some trouble in the form of long division,
but one day he'll discover the library, and Jean Genet,
and everything he's learned about the world will make sense:
why acupuncture means you can stick pins in people,
why it's better to have ten lollipops at once,
what 'Homo Erectus' really means,
and why the earthworm never needs to worry
if its slimy, willing neighbor
is a boy worm or a girl worm.

Jonah knows. Year after year,
we're breathing in the sparks of infinitesimal beings grinding away in the dirt,
just to spend their blind lives seeking a like-minded creature
with whom to mate.

For all our fractions and charts and tables, with every step
we're sharpening our stakes in the pulsing food chain
of love and perversity.

RUTH L. SCHWARTZ

READING MY STUDENTS A POEM

You don't have to understand it. You don't even have to listen.
Just think about kissing each other later, out in the parking lot,
while creatures that hide themselves in the daytime
gleam like grounded stars and rustle close.
Opossums with their trembling snouts,
eyes like burning cinnamon.
Foxes dashing through the ditches, tails like flags.
Think about pushing each other up
against slammed car-doors, cool hard metal;
think about opening mouths to each other,
deep enough to swim, ignoring all the signs—
Mine and Yours, His and Hers, His and His, Hers and Hers—
squirming with sibilance and swooning
underneath the June moon,
letting the line breaks
break you open. Just think about that.

RUTH L. SCHWARTZ

THE INTRODUCTORY POETRY CLASS
DEFINES RANCHERA

Jenna Riofrio, looking little like a cold river
with her blond-streaked hair, tight tank top
layered over bra straps of contrasting color,
says It's that music
you skip quickly past
as you look for the station you want. But
Yvette Monteflores says No,
ranchera is what you crank up high
in your pickup truck
with all the windows permanently
down. And Mary Lee McGough still wants to know:
Is it like folk, is it like country?
Then Jenna Riofrio, whose very name is a poem,
whose finest simile—coined to describe the grip
of a clothespin—was "tight as a virgin's legs
on Prom Night"—
emerging, in that instant, from her beautiful
boredom—then quickly mantling herself again—
and Yvette Monteflores, who wears glasses,
comes early, stays late, and holds inside herself
a flower-covered hill—
and Mary Lee McGough, who is fifty-six
and rather didactic,
but once read the class her riff on the word "French,"
which included French kissing
on the French Riviera—
bend to the waiting opened mouths
of their first odes.

RUTH ROUFF

LET MIKE DO IT

"What I need," said my
GED student Mike, "is
a little-ass book of
poetry. With rhymes."
Mike was talking with
another student. It's only
recently he's begun
talking to me. When he
first arrived in class,
he'd stare into space
as if placed on ice.
When I'd
instruct the class, he
wouldn't react.

But now I know
his Achilles' heel:
poetry. "What does
philosophy mean?"
he asked me the
other day. He's
assembling a storehouse
of words to
use in raps.

He keeps his
internal life under
wraps. Like a
true poet, he
exposes himself
slowly.

"Philosophy," I
said, "is what
you think about
life, or some other
important thing."

I don't want to
romanticize Mike.
He certainly has
his deficits, and
I've lost four
students already
this year.

Not dropped out. Dead.
My philosophy of
life is, "there's only
so much you can
do."

But I'll help Mike
find his little-ass
book of poetry

With rhymes.

JOSEPH ROSS

CONVERSATION AFTER CLASS 1

for B.M.

I listened carefully,
my furious chin seeming
to rest in my hand.

He told me of this assault
on the subway
two days before.

Four guys jumped him
after asking for his phone,
his seventy-five cents.

Who asks for seventy-five
cents in America?
It gets you laughter.

He sits before me today
with bandages around
a limping mouth,

his lips like cartoons.
He ought to have tweeting
birds circling his head.

He knew it was coming,
when it was coming,
he said.

He knew from the one
guy's look. This won't end
well, he said.
So, he told me, he took

off his shirt, knowing it was
too restrictive.

Here is a knowledge
I do not have
a degree in.

I have nothing
to heal this,
nothing but

seventy-five apologies
that America's morning
is a dawn

purple as the spreading
bruises on his
teenage back.

JOSEPH ROSS

ELEGY FOR A STUDENT

Kevin A. Nelson, 1985-2004

Because my teeth were clenched
for years after you

died, I kept a kind of respectful
silence when it came to writing

about you. I used your own poems
to remember the urgent fingers

driving your pen, the quiet fury
resting just above your eyebrows,

the unnamed sadnesses
swirling like ancient smoke

around your worried face.
But now, with the rainfall

of years, I am finally able to let
the sun loosen my mouth,

so that a word might pass through it
that will not choke me with bones.

There seems to be a general
easing of the sky around my teeth,

an opening of that tomb to light,
enabling me to remember

you as you were:
an eighteen year-old who died

with a pen in your hand and a parade
of poems walking out

of your mouth, which was not
clenched, but which was open

like a garden, splashing blossoms
into the waiting air.

RON RIEKKI

NOON IN THE GARDEN OF QUEER THEORY AND ALABAMA

Judith Butler on the board, not allowed
in their heads. I explain performativity,
how they're trick-or-treating right now
with their Dale Earnhardt Jr ballcaps
and clean jeans. I come to the next class
in a dress. A future Episcopal priest
in the back row looks like he just saw Satan.
I fill them in on Adam Isaiah Green
and Eve Kosofsky Sedgwick, their eyes
hot and teary, a few listening like God
might be in the room. There are fevers
in teaching, dangers. I will lose this job
but not before I make them aware
that the word "homosexual" appears
nowhere in the Bible, that it's a mistranslation,
that Jesus never speaks
the word, that they've all been lied to,
and I will not be replaced by *a man
who lies with a male* but rather will be
replaced by a man who simply lies.

ROMA RAYE

BIG FAT FAKER

I'm a faker.
A big fat faker.
A liar liar pants on fire
phony
fraud
faker.

I am an imposter.

I barely know what I'm doing most of the time,
and the rest of the time?
I'm making things up. It is not unheard of
for me to be reading the text selection for the first time
with my first period students feeling like a jackass
for assuming the lesson I got off the internet that morning
would actualize into something decent. Now, to be fair, I have moments
where I am prepared and ready to conquer
my sophomoric demons with inspired,
standard-guided instruction. But those are just moments, flukes,
like trying to slip through the worm hole in the time/space continuum.
A chance to see an alternate reality of what I could be,
if I wasn't such a goddamn faker.

Have you ever had one of those days where you're
standing in front of a room full of teenagers waiting for you to teach
them something only to fall head first into the chasm of
"Oh shit, I forgot to copy the answer key"
as soon as they've asked the first clarifying question regarding the handout
you have just handed out still hot from the Xerox machine?
Have you ever just stood there answering,
"That's an interesting question. What do you think about that?"
every time a student asks you something because you, yourself,

just barely understand what it is you're trying to get them to understand?

I didn't set out to become a teacher.
I never dreamed it would be me up there in front of the class.
I hated school. It was hard for me.
I was the fat kid with bad hair.
I never really fit in. Oh, I'm still a freak. Only now,
they've asked me to join all the
multi-cultural committees and anti-defamation leagues saying
"Don't you want to make the school
a better, safer place for all our students?"
and I'm like, "No. I'm just trying to make the school a safer place for me."
I'm constantly going off on tangents and forgetting
that I'm supposed to be in charge. I end up chatting with the students
about really interesting but completely random topics. They ask me
questions
I can't answer and the ones I want to try and answer?
I'm not allowed.

So, when a student says to me,
"Ms. E, I've been thinking . . ."
I know that I am doomed.
Doomed.
Because I am a faker.
A big fat faker.
A liar liar pants on fire
phony
fraud
faker.

DOUGLAS RAY

MORNING WHITMAN

April's seams (and seems) are fraying,
            bursting with ragweed, pollen, and hormone-
                        infused drama. We read Whitman
on the benches beneath an old oak,
            the fluorescent classroom too
                        institutional, too routine
for talk of "promontories," "filaments," and "souls."
            I ask a student to read, and he does so
                        in the persona of a hellfire, foot-washing
preacher, slapping his text at stanza breaks,
            throwing his cap off into the green, and then
                        collapses to the dewy ground (it's barely
8:15 a.m. and we're full throttle), slings his arms
            into a line and yells skyward, "I'm crucified!"
                        A half-rest later, another student
pipes up, "Is that apostrophe
            when the speaker addresses his soul? It's not
                        like it's going to answer, right?"

DOUGLAS RAY

CHAPERONING

At the dance for seniors, a wash of fuchsia
mint, pearl, silver, and general air of lust

and expectation, the music's not unlike
the pulse of downtown gay bars; the lights

distort everyone to beautiful. I see one
of the gays—beloved by his class—in profile

(he's experimenting with facial hair). He looks
tired and tense. His date's jacket is a year too big.

I ask him later how things are. He rolls his eyes, filled
with disappointment. I want to say, "Don't let another

guy ruin your anything," but I know that it's not the last
time that will happen. I want to say, "It will get better"

in five minutes, in college, in x or y, but things might not.
I adjust his violet bow tie that, really, needs

no attention (perfectly placed)—my hopeful gesture,
my pitiful blessing, for his good night.

AMANDA POWELL

WANTING THE GOOD

In 1992, the Oregon Citizens Alliance sponsored a ballot initiative to amend the state constitution to stipulate, "the Department of Higher Education and the public schools shall assist in setting a standard for Oregon's youth that recognizes homosexuality, pedophilia, sadism and masochism as abnormal, wrong, unnatural and perverse and that these behaviors are to be discouraged and avoided."

1.

My hand at your neck, *perverse*
our eyes finding each other along the pillow, *unnatural*
a smile begun before we're awake, *abnormal*
our bodies milky and sallow, freckled and still, *wrong*—

"Want to do something perverse and unnatural?" we grin
over the breakfast or supper dishes.

If you are squeamish, don't prod the beach rubble,
whispers Sappho, in Mary Barnard's translation, the only
help I have not to do myself in, *unnatural, wrong,* at sixteen

and drawn to a best friend's arms—lifetimes ago
to my students, some of whom must wonder too—
Sappho I had, and Anaïs dancing with June, who however
retreated to Henry Miller as night wore on.

2.

From twenty-six or -seven centuries past, from torn papyrus
and libraries burned, in high school I starred a fragment:

> *We shall enjoy it*

> *As for him who finds*
> *fault, may silliness*
> *and sorrow take him!*

3.

Not dreams, but those husks of near-sleep
buzz with my mind's exhortation (or one of my minds)
on its soapbox, claiming our right to live.
Yet another insomniac self hunches at headquarters, plotting
precincts, wards, towns, and counties, while another dials
long after other volunteers go home, calling
one more voter to explain finally
more than a right to live, but willing to thank her
whatever she says and get on with it, make the next call.
Another mind writes on night pages definitive
Letters to Editors. My beloved rests weary beside this campaign
until I get up to read, heat some milk, call a friend
back East where it's already morning.

4.

Silliness and indignation overtook a man
who jumped on his bicycle to chase you
out of the trailer park we leafletted
one showery Saturday; finding fault, he found
you at your most Franciscan, smiling
and thanking him, that's all, till he took off baffled
and I found you, shaking.
Each doorstoop done.

5.

The day arrives and we're at a polling place with signs, sun just risen,
my sweetheart and sister and I, "No on 9,"
outside Crest Drive Elementary, the requisite 100 feet from the doors,
as voters drive up and parents deliver
children to school. By far, the majority smile and wave.

One woman shrieks, from her car,
"I can't *believe* you'd do this in front of the children."

We continue to hold our signs and smile and not
make love in public, or throw things, or rage.

6.

In the dark the therapists wear white sashes
in case someone caves in if we lose.
—But we're not losing. Numbers rising,
counts in from the counties, a small steady margin for us

—and now they know for sure. And you my love
leap with your arms flung high and cheers
of a glee forty years at least
caught in your throat but freed now.

Sorrow wait out there.
We shall enjoy this.

7.

Why did we win?

Every call to a wavering voter,
each pamphlet dropped on a stoop, all
the neighbors stopping to chat, the ladies
on lunch breaks filling envelopes, talks
in temples and churches and school boards, but we
know why we won this round—three lemons and a new knife:

Never used, a knife you're prepared to throw away,
said my sister's godmother, who learned this in Somalia,
and it will work, but only for a good thing.
Why do I love you completely? Neurobiologists
hypothesize homo- and hetero-brains;
geneticists, genes; you've got the looks and you're
the wittiest person I know. The real reasons
are all here, walking into the woods

with three lemons and a cheap knife from Safeway,
up behind the cemetery, along a muddy back track
over fallen logs, under slow-dripping boughs

on November 3rd, after voting, across mosses, treading
the spiky, velvet, emerald, rusty softness, the twigs
that thread new generations through downed leaves,
hushed, until you find the perfect spot to do what she said.

We halve the lemons with the knife and throw them
where they won't be touched. In spongy earth
I bury the knife. We do it as it must be done, wanting
a good thing.
        That, and my sister's godmother's prayers
of intercession to the saints for this campaign,
and my mother's petitions with her congregation,
and your mother's Novenas to Our Blessed Lady,

these explain the balance tipped to a victory—
because science and faith agree, the truth

will out, eventually.

KENNETH POBO

NOOOOO

I'm teaching Greenberg's play *Take Me Out*.

A good time to come out—
how can we talk honestly about the closet
if I'm in it?

One student, a nice kid, says,
"Noooo, you aren't!"

"Yes, I am."

"Nooooo, you aren't."

Perhaps he wants me to rustle
up a tiara and start talking
like Richard Simmons.

I can't be gay and his teacher.

This is eastern Pennsylvania,
not San Francisco—

I can't be gay and his teacher.

He's not angry. Or superior.
It's just

not possible.

KENNETH POBO

TEACHING WALT

In grad school the Whitman
                                scholar
            taught Walt as a nice
            Str8 guy who loved nature
            and as for that stuff in   *Calamus*
            turn the page
            it might give the wrong
            impression to impressionable
            minds

One lazy Tuesday afternoon

            Walt himself came to class
            weary of hearing how he
            was a nice str8 guy
            who loved nature yes
            he did love nature and
            28 young men soused   with spray
            he would be happy

to take all our questions
and kiss them

NINA PICK

SCHOOL OF EMBODIED POETICS

When I first started teaching, I thought
my students could see my heart on my sleeve.
I thought they could read the footnotes of
a body splayed open as a book.
I felt embarrassed to have such a
visible heart; there was something shameful about
the whole goopy mess, its ungovernable pulsations,
its lightning blush. It seemed none of my students
had a heart like mine; their hearts were bundled
in their baggy sweatshirts like a packed lunch.
I stood up there on the first day and
dug my hands into my pockets, thinking I
could hide my heart and its waywardness.
I slumped my shoulders, faced the
the blackboard, shouted from
behind the projection screen.
But wherever I stood, my heart sparked
like a disco ball, doing
its unmistakable kaleidoscope dance.
I went to my supervisor: I'm so
embarrassed, I said. I think my students
are judging me harshly. They've probably
never seen such a heart before.
She shuffled papers, looked at
the results of my classroom observation.
She said, Well, the best you can do
is be a role model. Maybe they've never had the chance
learn about the heart. Try teaching it
the same way you teach grammar.
So I went back to class, and returned to
the living pulse of the text:
I glimpsed the luminous globe behind

the poem's dark ribs, felt its warmth streaming
through form, through syntax, through meter's
tangled orchard. I saw the poem as a latticework
interwoven with sun. Each sentence was
parsed by the light.
On the desks we drummed
the heartbeat of the iambs. My heart led an
orchestra of small flowers.

DONALD PERRYMAN

WAS MELVILLE ALSO GAY?

As a closeted English teacher
I heard the comment on occasion
standing before a bright-eyed class of teens,
almost always a boy blurting it out
in negative fascination: "That's so gay!"
Something in the lesson had struck him
as dangerously, grossly homoerotic—
Ishamel and Queequeg in bed together
or even two women declaring their love.
The boy's delicate, budding sense of self
straight (or more especially if not)
demanded that he distance
or at least appear to distance himself
from what felt just too queer
to let pass without his protest.

I'd always ask, as if I didn't know,
"What's that supposed to mean?"
"Oh, never mind, Mr. P," he'd say
and duck his lovely adolescent head,
not thinking to have triggered
my stock response, given as always
for what it could be worth:
"Is gay supposed to mean something bad?
It's not a choice or an illness, you know."
And then I might digress to say
that private beds were hard to get
in 19th century Massachusetts,
leaving unexplained that Melville,
so I'd heard, was closeted like me.
I always thought of the statistical one in ten
kids sitting incognito in that room

needing desperately to know
that someone with authority
thought being gay was perfectly okay.

Early one morning before first bell
Rick, himself a striking Billy Budd,
dropped by as he so often did
just to say hello and give me a hug
in the good old days before touching
a student in any form or fashion
was made into a punishable crime.
This time though he started weeping
in the safety of my tiny office space;
told me, reddened eyes aglisten,
the secret burden of his young years:
anal penetration forced on him
when he was 12 by another boy, 16.
No counselor I, but loving him
more than he'd ever guess or know,
I tendered my profuse compassion,
asked if the pain had been
physical too, besides emotional.
He said yes—he'd even bled.
It was, I assured him, a cruel crime,
but wondered if some of that pain
was the chronic, haunting thought
that sex between two males was wrong?
He said no (maybe only guessing
the answer I hoped he'd give)
that it wasn't because it was gay,
but just the awful fact that it was rape.

Before I'd ever heard about Herman
or even about myself in fact,
a state college undergrad,
I had an English paper to write
but couldn't decide between

Whitman's *Leaves of Grass*
and Melville's *Moby Dick*.
Dr. Davis, a gruff, congenial sort,
advised me as we strolled
from his world lit class one day.
"Do Melville. That's more like
something you ought to be
interested in studying."
I didn't ask and thus will never know
just why he steered me out to sea
from Whitman's Mannahatta.

SHANNON PARKER

(UNTITLED)

Yesterday after school,
I am at the bike rack.
There's a lot of maneuvering necessary
to get to the Fuji Crosstown my parents
found for me on Craigslist a few weeks ago
when I told them I was going to start biking to work.

I work to release it from among
the mostly-student bikes crowding the rack.
Above me is the din of students who aren't
quite ready to go their separate ways yet,
who are milling around, doing what middle school kids do
when they've been released by the final school bell.

From among the many voices, one catches my attention.
I'm not quite sure because it's loud and I have my back turned
and I'm struggling with my combination lock,
but I think I hear her say something like,
"That's the bad teacher, the lesbian."
I don't recognize the voice, but the way
she says,
"lesbian,"
that tone,
I do recognize.

I don't think it's one of my students,
but I can't be sure without looking
and something
keeps me
from turning around
to see.

You see, I'd already been feeling self conscious—

not because I'm a lesbian,
not because of the kind of teacher I am—
but because I feel like I look stupid
in my canary-colored helmet and my spandex bike shorts.
Because I'm overweight and out of shape,
and riding this new bike doesn't feel natural yet.
Because I feel wobbly and awkward and fat.

Suddenly, as I'm biking away,
I realize that I am feeling
like a middle school student
instead of a teacher,
remembering what it's like
to be called names—
not
"Lesbian"
then
or
"Dyke"
—names
like
"Piggy."

I realize that this is why
I didn't turn around,
didn't face the obvious disrespect being directed toward me,
didn't meet the gaze of a student who saw me
not as Ms. Parker, but as an other,
someone who was less than,
and whose feelings obviously didn't matter to her.

We all have things that make us feel
wobbly,
awkward,
and, if not fat,
then fill in the blank.

This is what I wish I'd turned around and pointed out to her.

ERIN NORTHERN

DIAGNOSIS

about a month into the relationship,
every partner I've ever had
has taken a big, huge, deep breath,
leaned in,
and kindly asked,
"has your ADD ever been diagnosed?"
and I suppose
that in the asking of this question,
they are actually not suggesting
that I see a neurologist,
or seek counseling support,
because they have, in fact, already concluded,
and diagnosed me as such

they have noticed
my inability
to successfully start a project
without procrastination,
or my ineptness of starting just one project,
instead of ten
or that I get anxious when they talk too slowly
to hold my focus
and impatient if they talk so quickly that I cannot process
all that is said
they have taken note of my poor social skills
the way my questions
are never painted gently into a scene
but instead are splattered across the canvas of conversations
and, of course, the fact that I don't always hear the last half
of what they're saying
because in my head,
I've already started engaging in five new dialogues at once,

have noticed the chill of the breeze in the air,
the way the light dances gracefully with the beauty in their eyes,
and yes, the sound of a train whistling in the distance

and I imagine how that train
was carrying an exhausted family,
a young girl
with the evidence of heartache spray painted on the palm of her hands,
a businessman
wearing a too-small shirt with stressed-out buttons
who has three perfect lines of a song repeating,
repeating, repeating in his head
but he won't give himself permission to sing
and that train is hugging
one small soul with tears drying hard upon his cheeks
due to the ice cream stain on the center of his shirt
and the way the boy-ness in his name has never laid peacefully upon his tongue

and I've wondered three times already
if they've even noticed yet
if they have noticed any of this
or if they're simply poised rifle chest high and at the ready
to deliver their diagnosis however,
incorrectly
instead of diagnosing me writer,
playful
imaginative
acutely focused
gifted with sensory
or diagnosing me,
teacher,
because at the end of the day,
teaching,
with thirty uniquely gifted minds intersecting simultaneously
into a cacophony of brilliance and creativity,
it's one of the few things that truly captures me,
and holds my attention

BONNIE J. MORRIS

RANDOM ACTS OF PROTECTION

for Frank Kameny

At nineteen, I came out, teen student in D.C.
And joined a talk show panel with Frank Kameny
When, from the fourth row, one man called out: *Sinners!*

A baby dyke who had not learned to fight, I learned from Frank.
I watched him duel our critic word by word,
Returning chapter blows, refuting verse,
Silencing a homophobe with swaggering precision;
His style a knife to carry against threat.

He was nobody's daddy, the father of the movement;
Nor some gorgeous prince, this king of our crusades and our protection.

His face front page as I walk, now, at fifty, with *The Blade's* news of his passing
And in the unexpected rain I use the unexpected news as my umbrella.
Frank Kameny protects me, one last hour.

Uncountable, the laws that bear his mark,
The freedom my torch carries from his spark,
The grief I feel to find his ember dark.

And into my now older, surging waters
Float students I have now grown to protect
This generation's out/proud sons and daughters
Whom I teach to grieve Frank with respect.

CARIDAD MORO

MAKING WEIGHT

In the teacher's lounge,
everyone worries
about the girl who just won't eat,
bones spiraling coral
beneath her forty-dollar
Abercrombie collar, gold bangles
banging against the stones
of her wrists begging feed me.

I alone notice the boy
at the wrestling meet—

weight down to the lowest class
he can stand, so he won't have to admit
he's not good enough
to hold anything down,
not even Gatorade
he dispels in spastic swirls
minutes before weigh-in.

I offer him my lunch, but
he insists he cannot eat
as he circles the trash cans,
wanting to dig among pizza crusts
and Pop-Tart wrappers
fluttering against the dark rim
of what others leave behind.

I watch him stalk the halls,
lettered and gorgeous, hunger-stained
teeth, shoulder blade axes
slicing through his skin,

ankles sharp as talons, game cock
jutting toward his next great meal
right before he takes the mat.

CARIDAD MORO

REFUSING THE ROTC PRESENTATION IN MY TWELFTH GRADE CLASSROOMS

It wasn't the boy I rejected
but his uniform—
pressed and starched
studded with stripes
and ribbons
beautiful
like the boy
out on furlough
not yet deployed
a façade
I could not allow
to unfurl
in the face
of the fact
that no soldier
humping through Kabul
ever looked
as good
or as clean
as he did
poised
to peddle
patriotism
and a life
he promised
they'd get to live
when they got back
from Iraq
or Afghanistan
where they wore
rumpled Earth
brown and green
duds they called
fatigues.

LISA L. MOORE

DO YOU HAVE TO BE GAY
TO TAKE THIS CLASS?

Of course. As you would know if you were in
the know, this is a singles bar where we gays
mingle, make the scene, find dates. *Of course
not.* I welcome students of all genders
and desires including none. But as
you may have heard you do have to be gay
to get an A. *Of course.* In this room you
will cherish embarrassment tenderly,
befriend the body's oddities and shame,
swell with delight in your own weird way.
By then, you either will or might as well be gay.

LISA L. MOORE

LESSONS FROM LGBT LIT

Alexander did not believe me
when I said Plato's ideal love
was between men. I thought, I know
what you want I know
you young man I have seen
your type before. You
will fight me as you fight
your own heart
you will fight me
I will fight for you
we will fight together
in the end
we will win.

In the end, I taught the class
from an undisclosed location
under armed guard.

In the end, I gave him a B
to never come back.
Maybe I taught him nothing
he taught me you can't win
em all over
you can't win
em all you can't win
I can't
make you love me.

STEPHEN S. MILLS

AFTER WE WATCH *THE HISTORY BOYS* IN CLASS, MY STUDENTS FEAR I WANT TO FONDLE THEM

Eighteen-year-old males take everything so literal. Their gay
        instructor shows them a film about a high school
teacher who cops a feel of his male students' genitals

while driving them home on his motorcycle, and they read
        this as I want to molest them, offer them a ride
in my Yaris, slip my hand over the gear shift, see what

they're packing in their skinny jeans. Of course they don't
        understand that it wouldn't actually be child molestation.
They're college kids, all over 18. The same age of the boys

in the movie, who willingly got on the bike, knowing what
        would happen. Found no harm in giving their
old teacher a thrill. When I tell my class this, they look at me

in shock, as if I've just said *fucking little kids is okay*. They're
        alarmed by this film. Ignore all other parts:
the discussion over education, over how one should teach,

learn, study. They've missed the whole point. When I ask
        why the seemingly straight boy would offer a blowjob
to the new, young teacher, they stare back dumbfounded,

and wonder if they must blow me to get an A. They want
        everything to be black or white, right or wrong,
gay or straight. Was I ever as naive as these boys?

I find it hard to remember a time I was truly shocked by sex,
        or the offer of a blowjob. A few months back a man
at least forty years my senior offered me one and I happily

accepted. Am I such an oddity? Will I soon be locked up?
        Put away for vulgarity? Like the Marquis De Sade,
forced to write poems with my own feces (hey, some guys

get into that)? Will I be fired? Told by some sobbing mother
        how her son felt emotionally abused by my film choice?
Will she wave her little heterosexual finger at me and say,

you can't have my son! Go recruit someone else? Will the son be there
        too? Curled into the fetal position, rocking
back and forth? I can see it now: *Gay Teacher Shows* The History

Boys In Hopes of Recruiting Young Males Into the Den of Homosexuality.
        If only it was that easy. If only I had that much
power, though pimply-faced boys with ADD and Zac Efron

haircuts aren't really my type. I think of my Art History professor
        in college, who was openly gay. A sweet older man,
who got accused of having sex with a minor, a 15-year-old,

but 20 years ago. Some boy he once knew, who convinced
        himself through therapy that he was "raped"
by a younger version of the man who taught me how to love art,

how to see it. I didn't believe it for a second. Felt sick
        to my stomach that such lies could surface
that many years later. Sick by how much the media

in the Midwest loves a good scandal that proves their own
        bigotry. He made a deal, fearing he'd be convicted
by a Kentucky jury of his supposed peers. A deal?

I'll never know for sure if he did it or didn't. Maybe what
        I'm trying to say is it doesn't matter.
We've set the boundaries, which change with time. And today

I must set my own boundary with this class full of fresh, but
        legal boys, who know nothing about sex, or the world,
or all the gray matter that makes up most of our lives. They don't

know if they should just suck it up, stay after class, flirt their way
        to A's, like the guy I had in class a few years ago,
who would lift his shirt from time to time, showing me his latest

cut or bruise from falling off his skateboard, but also revealing
        his well-toned torso. He'd tell me how he'd do anything
to pass the class. Was I tempted? Of course, he played well

into every teacher/student fantasy I've ever had, but much
        to his surprise he failed. For I am not Hector.
Not the old, lonely professor just yet. But it doesn't matter

because some of these boys can see me in no other way.
        They're terrified by my film, by my hands—hands
that might just feel good, might just confuse the senses. Yes,

they fear no matter what they do, they've already been recruited.

STEPHEN S. MILLS

ST. STEPHEN CONTEMPLATES SPEAKING TO HIGH SCHOOL STUDENTS ABOUT POETRY

A friend from college calls to ask me to be a guest speaker
    in the high school creative writing class she's teaching
in Terre Haute, Indiana, which is located near
    Saint Mary-of-the-Woods College founded
by Mother Theodore Guerlin, who is only the 8th "American"
    to ever be sainted (though she was born in France).
My friend says her students would like to hear
    from a published poet (which I truly doubt),
says I can do it over the phone from Florida,
    which might make it more exotic and enticing
to those landlocked youths. But what advice can I give?

Last week, I told a stranger in a gay bar I was a poet,
and he yelled into my ear, over the thumping bass:
    poetry is just a hobby, as if he thought he could convince me
over rum and cokes and pretty dancing boys
    that I was a fool and should get a real career. He shouted
over and over again that word: *hobby*,
    which makes me think of scrapbooking mothers,
my father in his workshop making wooden doorstops
    in the shape of turtles and pussycats,
and even of Saint Theodore who had a fondest for beaches,
    collected seashells as a child on the banks of the Atlantic,
and I imagine her disappointment when she arrived in the woods
    of Indiana in the 1840s, no ocean in sight.

I like to think she had a tiny wooden box with a vial of sand in it,
    like those key chains they sell in Florida
with the words: "My Beachside Property" stamped on them,
    and perhaps she had a few shells in the box too,
that at night she held to her ear waiting for the sound of the sea
    to drown out the roaring of untamed wilderness.

80

Shell to ear, she'd sway with the rolling waves of France,
        a sound that reminded me, as a little boy (shell to my ear),
of a toilet flushing, but she knew nothing of indoor plumbing,
        or the sound two men make getting off in a bathroom
stall in a gay club where the man screamed *hobby* in my ear
        five—maybe six times before I turned to his ear
and shouted: *fuck off*, which I can't tell the students of Terre Haute
        when they ask why I'm a poet.

I can't tell them no one will ever respect you. That it sucks
        most of the time, and nearly all poetry publications
don't pay. That it is, in fact, very much like being a nun:
        serving the greater good—or something like that.
Or maybe, it's just selfishness at its finest: *here read my poems*
        about me, me, me—how very un-pious.
I can't tell them how sometimes I wake in the night
        with a burning desire to feed all my poems to the dog,
who would surely vomit them back up all over the house,
        perhaps in revised versions that would win me some award
(this poem's already been regurgitated three or four times—
        what do you think?). I can't tell the students who spend
Friday nights in cornfields getting drunk,
        that I have a Master's Degree in Creative Writing,
yet no one will hire me, that people fear
        those who devote large amounts of time to activities
that will never make them money, or get them sainted.

        And because it will be over the phone
I can grit my teeth and say: *keep writing kids, never give up.*
        But I'd like to tell them the truth—
or some version of it: say how most of them will fail,
        will never write after they leave high school,
some getting pregnant, dropping out, others making it
        to college only to grow fat and become alcoholics
or religious zealots who go around attempting to banish
        anything they don't understand or don't have a quick
reference for in their revised version of God's Word.

I wonder if old Theodore was as stern and literal
as these Indiana conservatives. I bet she had more
        common sense, perhaps even a sense of humor,
and I bet some nights she cursed the God she loved.
        The one that let that robber murder her father
and made her become a nun—a virgin for all time,
        stuck in Indiana, far from the sands of France,
just like some nights I curse the God that made me a poet
        here in Florida where salt hangs in the air,
and there's always the distant sound of the ocean
        rushing to meet the land.

LUCIEN DARJEUN MEADOWS

ICARUS RISING

Every April you dream of flight, of spreading grey wings
against the rising sun, from your perch in the concrete
springhouse on the edge of campus. These rural fields
are filled with violets and hyacinth; sweet blooming weighs
the air with the Gordian scent of memory, for you remember

when you were a girl, arriving on campus in a long skirt;
when you changed majors, homes, your body. Now, you
spend evenings dreaming of a figure with scars that flare
like thorns where roses once bloomed, of a new world

where streets are filled with soft prismatic smoke and white lights,
where you are known only by your new name. Across the wide
meadow, the laughter of children echoes in the lonely room
where you stand caught between light and shadow. Your body

aches from moulting layers. Hot official wax seals the conclusion
of your refuge, your paraffin cocoon dissolves, and wings
burst from your skin, wings that will never betray, never melt.
Outside, the dawn is singing, and you step out, your hair afire.

PABLO MIGUEL MARTÍNEZ

FRAGMENT 16

This year little is sweet
for young ones like María Espinoza
the road between Now and Then

is strewn with thorn and stone
She asks *Sir, did she really live
on an island called Lesbos?* The boys

laughed when we got to Sappho, laughed
because they don't believe
anyone could be from such a place

they can't believe a woman
would want less than their new tautness
to call her Love. But in her

sure butchness María senses that
a woman's heart a woman's thought
a woman's eyes are the finest things

in this wide world. Like Sappho
María knows that though
Some men say an army of horse and some men say an army on foot

*and some men say an army of ships is the most beautiful thing
on this black earth* Sappho said it is
what you love

This is what María feels
this dismembered year
She walks out

into an afternoon
teeming with youth and doubt
I know María will scrape

her soul's elbows too
many times to count
but through it all this girl

will carry that fragment
remembered perfectly by heart
remembered there like the one she will love

TERRY MARTIN

THE THIRD WRESTLER CRIES

Never the football players.
Never the basketball players.
No baseball or track or soccer guys.
Only the wrestlers.

Jaime is the third.
Freshman coiled tight as a spring,
biceps bulging under t-shirt sleeves,
here during my office hour wanting
to talk about the Sherman Alexie poem
he has chosen for his class presentation.

All earnestness, gaze direct, he practices
reading it aloud, knee bouncing
up and down like a jackhammer.
When he reaches a line that moves him,
lips tremble and he halts, unable to continue.
Brown eyes look up at me, liquid pools
teeming, startled fish about to spill over.
"See, I *get* this guy" he tells me, voice cracking.

Jaime, I think, I'm not as hungry as you,
spitting and sweating and starving away
those last three pounds, trying
to make weight by Thursday.
Not as tired as you,
dark circles ringing your eyes.
But believe me: *I get you, too.*
See, I know about intensity—
its blessing and its curse.
Know the pressure of one-on-one,
how it feels to be alone out there,

on the mat, in the spotlight,
facing that next opponent.
Confident and unsure.

And isn't the point to love—
even if too much, or the wrong way?
To lose yourself in what you do
in hopes of finding yourself?
Listening, nodding, I shove
the Kleenex box across the desk,
offer the tissue.

TERRY MARTIN

GIVING THE TEST

"We have to do all that we can to build ourselves up.
In these trying times we live in, all that we have
to cling to is—each other."

— *Tennessee Williams*

Pens scratch across white, leaving tracks in snow.
Meghan hunches, forehead in hand, squints at the marks,
deciphering. Fabian sighs, shoots me a glare
that says "This is all your fault, you know."
Jeff looks up at the ceiling,
Julie stares out the window,
Cody taps his pen.

Watching them, I think of the narrator of this play,
who's a character in it, too. Insider and outsider,
like I am here, slipping and sliding in and out of the margins.

I love these damaged characters,
burning with the fires of human desperation,
mirroring each of us in their dignity and tragic beauty.
The controlling mother, making plans and provisions,
unwilling or unable to face the facts. Stuck in the past,
she clings to what she can never have again.
A daughter, too fragile to move from the shelf,
limping along in painful self-consciousness.
The absent father, a telephone man
who fell in love with long distance.
The emissary from the outside world, one brief breath
of fresh air for this closed-off, musty family.
The trapped son, nailed into a premature coffin.
His desire for freedom in the midst of duty.
To save himself, he must act without pity,
but he will be haunted by this for the rest of his life.

It's the larger questions that interest me, ones too big
for this one small exam. But they're eighteen years old.
And we've got fifty minutes. So we do the best we can.
The real test, the one I can't give, but that
will be given, will ask harder questions:
In what ways are you "crippled" or fragile?
What have you lost? What do you miss?
Where are you clinging too tightly?
Is just a little happiness and good fortune
too much to ask for? Is it enough?
Have you felt, or do you feel, trapped in some way?
What must you do to save yourself?
Do you have regrets that haunt you?
("If not yet, you will," I want to tell them).

Laurie's eyes wander toward Michael's paper.
She catches my stare, squirms, regains her focus.
Miguel's left knee bounces up and down,
while Nicole searches for the right words
at the bottom of her Starbucks cup.
They are remembering a world
where everything happened to music.

My affection for them washes over the room
like a slanted beam of light.
I wish you luck—and happiness—and success!
All three of them—

JEFF MANN

COUNTRY KIDS

Other than those students courageously,
openly queer, they are my favorites,
the country kids. They hail from Wytheville
and West Virginia, Woodstock, Southside,
the Blue Ridge, the Shenandoah, the hills
of Craig, Pulaski, Botetourt and Giles,
with their muddy cowboy boots, chunky
belt buckles, trucker caps, blessedly
impeccable manners, Southern vowels
slow and broad as mine, boys with
their bushy-handsome goatees, girls
with their big hair and tight jeans, telling
tales of four-wheeling and deer-hunting,
the time some well-off snot from the DC
suburbs made fun of their local accents,
called them ridge-runner or hillbilly.
I am less than the slick, urbane professor
they might expect (loafers, ties, corduroys?)
with my own camo baseball caps, cowboy
duster, scuffed boots and Rebel beard, eager
passions for Southern food and pickup trucks.
I am more than the mountain man I appear,
joking about my lust for country-music star
Tim McGraw, often mentioning my partner
of many years, explaining what the bear-paw
and Lambda tattooed into my left biceps signify.
Southern Baptist and right-wing Republican
many of them might be, yet we feel so much
at home together that they bring me ramps
and deer jerky, creecy greens, kudzu jelly,
raspberry moonshine, all the rural delicacies
that delight the redneck heart, gifts of
a shared and honest fondness that might
turn toward change, quietly political.

JEFF MANN

GALLERY, VIRGINIA TECH

Thank the Goddess
they're still around
these cocky little butch
girls with their flannel
shirts work boots tattoos
softball caps the very breed
of buddy-women who got me
through the aching loneliness
of my youth Braver than
I ever was at that age
Jess sits in the back of
my creative nonfiction class
and reads aloud about
coming out to her mother
Mary shares a sonnet in poetry
workshop about wanting
to marry her lover despite
the backward/devout state
of Virginia and I want to
take them both out for
several pitchers of beer
and barbequed racks
of ribs, later to confess
—despite my leatherbear
penchant for bearded boys
bound down to beds—
my decades-long infatuations
with Jane Seymour
and Jessica Lange.

*

She sidesteps pronouns
in her essays mentions

BDSM and pansexuality
in her midsemester journals
dark-haired Goth already
what we Southerners
would call "fine-looking"
her face red her voice
quavering with rage
as she describes for
her fellow students how
little voice or freedom
women in her family have
I want to escort her into
the bright world of
strong Sapphos I know
show her meadows
islands mountains
where women are heard
Instead I show her
web sites listing MFA
programs, give her a copy
of Dorothy Allison's
Two or Three Things
I Know for Sure.

*

Mars and Mercury
let me be the ferocious
father totemic bear
furry and fanged
guardian of the tribe
guiding the young selves
I used to be through
the gauntlet of fire and fear
and jibe Let one prayer
be not selfish and wasted
but selfless and fulfilled

RALPH MALACHOWSKI

ADJUNCTIVITIS

Professor, you find all my mistakes, then mark them wrong.
        You're so mean.
This week's reading assignment made my head hurt.
So what if Shelby Steele isn't a woman? She should be.
        Shelby is a girl's name.
No. You can't come in late, take a cigarette break and leave early every class.
To do group work in class, you must attend class.
I can't afford to buy the textbook.
"My advice to you is to ask your student why he wrote
        Mike Unt and *Bend Over Sucker* for two of his answers on your
        quiz. Perhaps he doesn't understand what those words mean."
"You expect too much intellectual prowess from your students. Next time,
        forget *The New Yorker*."

Harold Bloom is an anti-semite.
Harold Bloom hates all women.
Harold Bloom is a racist.

White people are racists.
Black people are victims.

Harold Bloom is old, and ugly and stupid.
From the film clip we saw in class, Julius Caesar looks old, ugly and stupid.
Who's James Mason? Who's John Gielgud?
Shakespeare is dead and buried and boring.
I don't have an answer. I'm tired.
Like many things in life, just showing up for class counts for much.

It's too hot in here.
It's too cold in here.
I don't like her.
I don't like him.

I don't think I should know those things.
If you don't believe everything President Bush says, you're a traitor.
If Gore Vidal isn't married, is he some kind of Democrat, *or worse?*
Something I don't like about this class? Yeah, some of my classmates.
"In the Kitchen," by Henry Louis Gates, Jr. is all about hair.
Jamaica Kincaid is just so sweet.
Shakespeare was a man who lived and died a long time ago.
Shakespeare isn't relevant today.
The only time Shakespeare is relevant is when someone
      like Leonardo DiCaprio makes it real.
The story you told us to read was so totally not interesting.
I could not understand one word in that article.
The guy who wrote that article is a bad writer.
Is the guy who wrote that story you made us read dead?
I'm not a Protestant, so why should I read anything this Calvino guy wrote?
Does the guy who wrote our textbook know what he's talking about?
      Can you prove it?
A lot of people think the author knows what he's talking about,
      that's why it's the eleventh edition.
You only repeated that twice today. Can you say it again?
The New Yorker isn't a real magazine.
If I can't find parking, how can I be late? It's not my fault.
Will I ever need to know this stuff again?

I don't understand . . .

The textbook costs too much.
I think we would do so much better on our next test if you would
      give us the answers first.
I didn't do the assignment because I didn't have the time.
Tell me what I should do. Should I bother to rewrite my paper?
Are you going to be a regular guy and pass me, or are you going to act
      like a *real* teacher?
Your textbook is so expensive. Should I bother to buy it? Will I ever need it?
Can't I e-mail my paper to you whenever I have the time?
I got through high school without using the library once.

ED MADDEN

AIRPORT SECURITY

At customs in the Dublin airport, flying
home, I stand in the passport line, alone.
An American immigration officer checks
my passport, looks me over, asks how long
I'd been there (two weeks), asks the reason
for my trip (research), asks me what
I do (teach college), smiles, says,
"I don't know how you do it. Must be hard,
working around all those cute girls."
He smiles, moment of male bonding with me
in airport security. I pause, his smile disarming.
"Actually, it's the cute boys who'd be
the problem." It takes a moment. He laughs,
looks again, stamps my passport, waves me on.

ED MADDEN

VBS

Every day, something to make,
something to color, a page to take home.
Later, there'd be store-bought cookies.
Later, there'd be Kool-Aid or punch.

I was Aunt Maxine's helper
for summer Vacation Bible School.
I helped the little girls with stickers.
I helped the little boys with crayons.

Sometimes we'd use glue and glitter,
or make something with tongue depressors.
Later, there might be a puppet lesson.
Later, there'd be prayer and songs.

We'd sing, *Roll the gospel chariot.*
Or, *The B-I-B-L-E.*
Or, *Be careful little tongue.*
Sometimes I got to lead the songs.

I was the boy teacher's helper,
the only boy among the girls.
Sometimes, I'd get to tell the story,
and sometimes use the flannel board.

The men had beards and flowing robes.
Joseph's face was young and smooth.
Joseph's coat was a woven rainbow.
My face was smooth, though not for long.

ED MADDEN

POSTCARDS

teaching summer creative writing camp
two weeks after my father's death

Morgan is writing a postcard to her grandmother
on the back of an old photo of a baby
in a chair, about how she'd read to her
when she was little—Savannah, too, writes
her dead grandma. "Sometimes, I am a lonely

boy," she writes. "Sometimes, a kite on the wall."
We're writing postcards to the dead or distant
today. Hannah wants to write to God,
Teddy to Obama, and some make up dead friends,
flowers at the grave, all that. But when

Morgan writes, "Sometimes, I'm still that baby
in the chair," I think of how my father
could make me feel so small, and think how small
he seemed, how small he was, near the end,
when I'd sit beside his bed, read to him.

KERRY MacNEIL

SOMETIMES

Sometimes, we recognize a thing because of its familiarity.
We recognize the slant of light on a page,
on a street corner,
on a curve of driftwood.
Teaching is like this
for me.

It is walks the width of the island of Manhattan, up near the top,
west to east,
from Fort Washington to Amsterdam,
to the same sagging,
aging
building I've loved
in everday-ness
for now,
improbably,
nineteen years.

Sometimes, we know a thing not by its contours and ridges and cadences;
sometimes we know a thing by what it is not.

This is not a two year service gig.
Not something until I sort myself out.
Not an accident.
Not a fluke.
This is not a place-holder until
grad school
law school
med school
business school.
Not
for me.

This is (and has been) a series of confounding lists.

This is being welcomed into a community that is
achingly familiar,
that smells like *pan de agua* and *café con leche* in the morning,
like *berenjena, arroz y habichuelas* at lunch,
and sometimes like incense from the *botánica* before dinner.
This is livery cab rides
and some Spanglish
and the making of a longed-for school,
where I would send my own beautiful, wise daughter,
if she weren't (right to be) so stubborn.

This year is reading
Julia Alvarez
Sandra Cisneros
Edwidge Danticat
Norton Juster
and E.B. White
in the hall, mostly.

This is not Lawrence, Massachusetts,
where my teachers pretended not to notice whiteness
and queerness.

This is other queer mums who
meet me
and read me
and render me
hushed and humble.

This is queer kids,
a fey boy and his best girlfriend-not-girlfriend,
who hold forth
and whom I need to rein in,
daily.

This is ten
and twelve
and fourteen-hour days
in the opening of this longed-for school
and being breezily outed by a colleague,
whose good intentions after the fact meant nothing.

Sometimes, we recognize the slant of light on a page in an old
(finished when my great-grandmother was five,
seven years before she came to Lawrence, in 1898)
train station that used to have a ticker board that clicked arrivals and
departures
       and tracks;
on a street corner where someone we love used to live;
on a curve of driftwood in a childhood photograph.

And sometimes we know a thing by its lack, by what it categorically is not.

HADAR MA'AYAN

ON BEING A QUEER
MIDDLE SCHOOL TEACHER

I write her up for not turning in her homework.
In response, she grabs the lunch detention slip,
Flips back long brown hair,
Stares me down with deep brown eyes
"I know you're a lesbian," she spits at me
Before storming out of the classroom

And that is the insecurity of being a queer middle school teacher.
You never know when it will be used as a weapon against you.
I have my own policy of discretion,
Born out of a fear for survival in my chosen profession
My own form of "don't ask, don't tell"
I don't volunteer to students that I am queer
Unless they come out to me first.
I don't lie or hide if asked directly.
And I am always out to my colleagues and administration.

As the words hovered in the classroom
"I know you're a lesbian"
The room full of middle school students waited,
Some tittering,
In that moment of choice, I could have said, "She's right"
Or "Let's discuss"
Or "Does anybody have any questions?"
But instead the fear rose in me
And I shrouded myself in a cloak of silence and said,
"Let's all get back to work,"
Knowing full well that I was running away
From the work that needed to be done.

RAYMOND LUCZAK

A BENEDICTION

in memory of Laurent Clerc (1785 – 1869)

Roiling across the Atlantic Ocean
to a country you'd never seen before,
you learned English on the ship over.
You were coming to America to teach
a deaf girl named Alice Cogswell.

Every day on the ship you kept a diary,
practicing English and wondering.
You taught Thomas Hopkins Gallaudet
the language of signs which you'd used
at the *Institution Nationale des Sourds-Muets*.

You brought together a group of seven students
that spring of 1817. Their eyes went afire
when they discovered how clear you were.
Many more would join them and listen to you.
Your hands were manna from the heavens.

Your signs, the true gospel of clarity,
freed so many souls ensnared
in low expectations and menial jobs.
They were shocked that the key to Heaven
was not in the Bible, but in their own hands.

Today not enough people whisper your name
in reverence. I light a candle in your honor.
There is no god greater than language,
and no greater evil than words twisted
just to deny others of lives rightfully theirs.

Let us all join hands and pray
that others will redeem the incredible beauty
of lives and signs not their own,
and that we will all run free
as gazelles pronking on the plains.

NATHAN ALLING LONG

JOURNAL

A student from fall semester has left
her journal in my office all year through.
It's a new year, so I tear out the rest
of her pages I once read and responded to.
She was a good student—not the best.
She always appeared like something was wrong,
but worked hard, turned in essays, finished tests,
and answered me in class when called upon.
I keep the blank pages so I can write
a journal, a sonnet sequence, or just notes.
But nothing I try turns out exciting
till I look on the last blank page, this night,
and see a line, in pencil that she wrote:
"Personally, I've never liked writing."

NATHAN ALLING LONG

WHITMAN'S GHOST

We had gathered, we thought, in a hotel
conference room to read to each other broken,
perfect poems, and to begin to tell
our stories, to share some words—blank tokens
of our lives—with a hundred other strangers.
One man spoke of taking his wife
out of the freezer (It's one of the dangers
of having an open mic—but that's life).
And when that poet was finally done
he surprised us, when he paused, then said,
"Allen Ginsberg died today." Everyone was stunned
silent. It was as if we all were dead.
Then the audience rustled and turned. From nowhere,
into the room flew a wild sparrow.

TIMOTHY LIU

ARS POETICA

I feel lucky to have published books.
To have royalty checks made out
in my name every third or fourth year
when the ledger balance creeps above

twenty-five dollars. To have been
awarded prizes no one on e-harmony,
gay romeo or match.com has heard of.
Perhaps they're jealous I get paid

for doing nothing, for teaching
my students they too might get paid
for doing nothing, shelling out
enough tuition to finance a house

they won't be able to afford. Call that
a pyramid scheme or a ponzi scam,
Avon or Am-Way, it's all the same.
Some say Creeley's load at the end

of a long career at SUNY Buffalo
was 0-0. Only a poet could get paid
for doing absolutely nothing, realizing
the very thing the founding fathers

envisioned as the American Dream—

G. M. LANG

WHITMAN GOT HIS GROOVE THANG, GROOVE THANG

My students are all over Whitman,
sliding up and down his electric body,
marveling at his scapula and neck-slue,
running a slow teasing finger round his nipples,
tittering at his man-balls, exulting
in the limpid jets of his hot tub of love,
wondering where the penis went.

Not truly an omission,
the "root" deception was also
no oversight, was deliberate, of course,
a management decision:
classroom, poem,
you run them much the same:
most every class and poem
has at least one penis,
male or female,
large or small,
useful, functional,
lots of fun,
often in the way,
the member
who scarcely needs mention
to be aroused,
and stroked,
won't be able to sit down
all morning.

SARAH-JEAN KRAHN

SYMPTOMATOLOGY OF AN IMPOSTOR

*As a strategy of survival, gender is a performance
with clearly punitive consequences.*

– Judith Butler

–You call yourself an instructor when
the dept. classifies you as a T.A.;

–you fret over how to pretend you
know what you're talking about but
fifty minutes fly by when you talk about

–Feminist Theory
is too subjective they say;
Queer Theory is as pointless
as "Working-at-McDonald's Theory";

–which is technically probably what
constitutes Marxist, but you weren't
the "instructor" then and

–to the queer question you probably would've said "No" while
philosophizing about how isn't everyone, really, queer?;

–your fellow "instructor's" student informs
you of the women's dance this weekend,
asks: "You are queer, aren't you?" to which you reply
"Um . . . yes?";

–you're not a dancer or a crowd-pleaser and no one
dances with you; silly
to think maybe *she* would take you
to the floor and show you how it's done;
student instructs teacher; maybe

107

they all know you're a fraud in your faux
hawk and camo pants; no different
than the het clubs your best girlfriend used to drag
you to: "Oh, I thought you two
were, you know,
together"

about which you think, "She's not my type," but at the long-awaited news
you're bi her first reaction is, "I'm unavailable."

/

MIODRAG KOJADINOVIC

A WORKDAY IN CHINA

Take off my web surf seducer mask,
wipe off the lazy lounging from the
corner of my eyes, jump into baggy
mid-calf length pants, smile at the
middle-aged man in the mirror;
go teach.

The classroom is just ten minutes away,
six floors down from my penthouse flat,
three hundred meters walk around the
pond, and another four floors up, for
we got the furthermost room, atop the
old library, from which one can see afar,
but where doors do not close properly,
and where in summer otherwise loud
clatter of fans is inaudible over the noise
of cicadas.

Work is hard, work is fun. I teach. I did
it in Europe, I did it (in a way) at the
western edge of the Americas, I do it
in Southern China. Half of my students
watch attentively, a few impatiently
interrupt throughout; a few doze, tired
with a heavy schedule. I need silence
to envelop me, safe as a womb, but
I talk.

I ask questions from the textbooks about
drugs and suicides and losing weight,
about Chinese festivals and the weather
in Scotland, the rise of Roman Empire

and the fall of imperialism, and about
a pet bear left in the car blowing a horn,
which perplexed a teetotaller. Maslow's
Hierarchy of Needs is easy for my students,
but *Language Learning Strategies* confuse
them.

When they answer correctly, I praise them,
when (again and again) I get no answer,
I visualise the distant coasts of my two
continents that I try to bring closer to my
students.

Teaching is magic, teaching is a bore. I work
hard. I enjoy my time. I explain Intercultural
Communication, I ask about divorce and
raising kids out of marriage, just as the
fellow-teaching couple from the other end
of the campus, who designed the book
as a freelancing project thought we all
should do.

I eat exotic tropical fruit grown locally,
I listen to the odd dialect of Nanning,
uttering Mandarin words the Cantonese way,
I go to the parks, I go to the hot springs, I
travel to Hanoi by bus and to Guangzhou
by plane.

I plan my days so I can go to the other
end of town and buy some cheese once
a fortnight, in the only small shop in
a city of two million that sells it. And all
the time I dream of a roof terrace in Lisbon
(in the inaccessible Fortress-EU)
overlooking the estuary, where I could
delight in life until one distant day, decades

110

from now (when work has worn me out),
as invisible seagulls screech high above,
breaking the solemn silence I yearn for,
I lay down myself to sleep/peace/silence,
Eternal.

JEE LEONG KOH

PARAGRAPH

I tell my VI graders my favorite word is *freedom*.
It is a house with many rooms on a lazy afternoon,
and outside the house an overgrown path runs
to the woods, where a speckled stream giggles.
I tell them *freedom* is made up of two syllables.
The first sounds like the neighing of a runaway
horse, unbridled muscles in his voice. The second
echoes like a blow on the taut skin of a tomtom.
And freedom, as all musicians and writers know,
is impossible without the discipline of the drum.
My students are impressed by my improvisation.
They turn to writing their paragraph with a will.
I look out the window of this old school building
and there's the river, sunlit, rippling green silk,
heading towards the sea. I don't tell them the sea.
Or what becomes of a carthorse with no master.
Or an abandoned house. I gently strike the drum.

JEE LEONG KOH

TALKING TO KOON MENG WHO CALLED HIMSELF CHRISTOPHER

Having been thrashed by the Express boys
in soccer, we retreated to the canteen.
You sitting with a foot up on the bench
challenged them, "Basketball tomorrow, we
sure won't lose. All-Star China versus England."

Ben smiled and said, "Whenever," to me, "Thanks, Sir,
for playing. A good game," and left for class.

Jin Sheng who christened himself Nicholas
yawned loudly, "School so *xian*, so boring, ah-h-h."

In the still air, you spoke your thoughts aloud,
"You know what, T'cher, I miss the Express class
by four points only," holding up four fingers.
"In prim'ry school, I very good boy one.
I every day go home and study hard,
practice my math, believe or not."

                    Jin snorted.

You cast a sidelong glance at me before
continuing, "But I did not make it, so
I turn bad. Sometimes got caught, *ganna* caned.
We run round in class, never sit down one."
No one could stop you. When they sent you out,
"We feel dem proud, laugh and walk out like nothing.
If I do very well and get five As
and behave, can I still go Express now?"

"No." I explained, "They take different subjects."

"I miss by four points only, now can't change.
English last time no good."

                      "T'cher, he like Shirlene,"
Jin sniggered. "You know her? From Three Express."

"I taught her in Sec. One. She did quite well
and moved from Normal to Express. She's nice."

"See, people very smart one. You no hope."

"Who say no hope? Maybe we meet in Poly."

Remembering my teacher's pledge, I said,
"That's right. Do well in your Four N exam,
go to the Engineering Institute,
do very well there and you can then go
to Polytechnic. It just takes a little
longer," anticipating your objection.

You said nothing. You lay down on the bench,
sighed very loudly and stared at the ceiling.
"School very xian," you said at last.
                              The bell.
"What period now?"

                  "Shit. Civics," Jin Sheng said.

"That arsehole Mr. Mah. I have no book,
sure *ganna* scolding one. Whole period. Fuck."
You peeked at me and quoted with a smirk,
"We use vulgarities a lot because
we have a limited vocabulary,
right, T'cher?"

Before I could reach for an answer,
you stood up, stretched and sauntered back to class.
The canteen grew quiet enough to hear
you in my head, without the need to translate
into imperfectly received pro-NOUN
see-A-shen curses at your gain and loss.
My *Caliban*, I thought, hurrying to
Lit class, *Pygmalion or* . . .
                    Your voice challenged,
"What, T'cher?" and I answered, "Christopher."

GEORGE KLAWITTER

VERNOUDI

We got him after he retired from Warren Easton,
Lee Harvey Oswald's old high school
where, rumor had it, the kids hung Vernoudi
out the window one day. Funny how I like

to think of him dangling there, his feet
far above the bougainvillea and oleander,
his white hair going whiter in the sun,
the New Orleans heat boiling in his ancient veins.

Well, over he came to us with his wooden compass
and a tongue nasty enough to suck through steel
on the horde of boys who sat at Holy Cross
waiting to see if this old guy could teach geometry

any better than torrid Brother Vincent who'd been at it
forty years already in the same classroom, wearing,
so we thought, the same black habit and shoes,
doing Euclid rote by rote, angle by angle.

Vernoudi had his favorites, as all teachers are not
supposed to have but do anyway. Valery Cavalier was
his special prey, every day up at the board
with his vigorous red hair to be embarrassed

by the vicious heart of the man who returned to the boy
every filthiness meted out to him for years on end,
every scream his mother screamed at him,
every smash his father landed on his head.

Valery was a beauty, but not above the tears which came
nearly every time he was forced to parade

his lack of geometric skills while the rest of the boys
snickered at his fate, praying they would not be next.

Valery was gay. We didn't know. But did Vernoudi
sniff it out? The red-haired martyr died of AIDS
half a century later and was buried in a cemetery
lost to Katrina's hungry hungry heart.

Even in death the boy's humiliated, washed down
the Delta to a Gulf where little fish await him
and take him home, recycled not for stars
but for our mother-water, the loving one,

the only one who understands that Valery
belongs among the great ones of the Deep,
at last the prince. He always was, no doubt,
the secret lover of our adolescent hearts.

GEORGE KLAWITTER

NICHOLAS

A little rag of sunshine
in our department, he danced across
the papers of various desks
like a cat needing our protection.
I kept my great arm around him
all the time, but Grecian cat
that he was, he thought himself invincible.

In Milton class he sat as quiet
as the Parthenon, his great dark eyes
darting here and there, his great dark mind
replaying the details of his latest fuck
or mapping out the strategy of his next.
He rarely spoke, but his Mediterranean laughter
brightened every corner of every room.

One cold day he surrendered into pain
and lay a mass of tangled thoughts
across a rumpled bed of pink percale.
Cruising in and out of sleep, he never stopped
the flow of happy syllables that comforted
his guardians and pacified the demons of his light
until one night it flickered and went out.

GEORGE KLAWITTER

A LETTER TO MY STUDENT

When I navigated the back streets
of New Jersey's Camden looking
for the cemetery that boasted
Whitman's self-designed tomb,

I never thought that thirty years
later I would be a Whitman too,
but a different Whitman,
not as brazen, more than brazen.

I had already done his house,
the one on Mickle Street,
not the one decaying sadly
on Stevens Street a block away.

I had seen his chair and slippers,
his stuffed parrot, the bed
he died in, his bathing trough,
even his prim outhouse in the back yard.

I had saturated myself in
the living remains of good old Whitman,
even had my photo taken out front,
jauntily, hand on hip like Whitman.

So, filled with the living, I sought out
the dead, found the cemetery,
dreary under a little rain.
I drove the rental car around the paths.

Away from all the other graves,
quiet on the side of a motionless tarn,
the grey granite little house
poked its way up into small trees.

I parked and went to the tomb-house,
looked in through the iron grate
at shelves of tombs, and there
among the rest rested the Good Gray Poet.

Alone at last with the old gay bard,
I felt as close to him as I'd ever get,
snapped a photo and culled a leaf,
then traced my way back out into Camden.

Whitman loved men, young men,
streetcar conductors and stevedores,
men of the people, men to impel
his solitary exultant verse.

And so I too depend on you,
football player and poet-to-be,
to throw my soul to the clouds
where I have not been in fifteen years.

There I gather my metaphors
and spin them into lines that celebrate
you, beard and shoulders,
eyes and steel-twisted arms.

If you were not singing in my heart,
I would not sing in words,
and the summer would die in a whimper,
bloodless, lacking the verve of juices.

You go on retreat, holying yourself,
somewhere south of the city,
on a ranch where the horses
dissipate the hay and your energy.

I stay behind and count the days,
knowing an hour with you
is Whitman's hour with Peter Doyle,
over and over across the years.

You age like a soldier, from the waist up,
and your ginger hair swims in the wind,
as your heart hungers for meaning
in a world tipping to dissolution.

If I ever gave up on life
it was because you were not here,
a gift to the heat and the drought
of Texas and my heart.

When you pasture your questions
in my cluttered mind, ideas
meld to a firmness and words
find a stallion to ride into meaning.

The autumn descends, slowly pushing
the summer sun into memory,
bringing cool to my ardor,
hardening it into permanence.

You are part of my being,
a part of the soul we share
now, yesterday, and into the eternity
I wish for, hope against hope.

CAMDEN KIMURA

MY MOTHER TEACHES HER STUDENTS ABOUT HEARING LOSS

My mother teaches her preschool students about hearing loss.
She shows them her purple hearing aid and
teaches them a song about a deaf elephant.
She takes pictures with her hearing-impaired students,
both of them showing off their hearing aids,
so they know that their music teacher is just like them.

My mother teaches neurodiverse students.
She used to work as a music therapist and now,
as a music teacher, she is delighted to have autistic students
in her classes. She calls them "her people" and is attuned
to their mood when the music gets too loud.
She shows the other students how easy it is to love their
non-neurotypical peers; even if they sometimes act differently,
they all sing the same song about a little autistic moose.

My mother teaches her students respect when they all reach
for the same drum at the same time. She teaches
her students patience when they sing long songs.
She teaches her students diversity when she shows them
instruments they've never seen: bagpipes, djembes,
a double bell euphonium.

My mother does not teach her students about homosexuality.
She does not teach them songs about same-sex penguins
falling in love. She does not take pictures with her gay students
and she cannot anticipate or account for their needs.
She cannot delight in the presence of gay students in her
classes because she does not know who they are and
they do not know that their music teacher is just like them.

COLLIN KELLEY

NIGHT RIDE HOME

Tonight, on the way home from teaching a poetry workshop, the wind tries to take my car, buffets the windows, steers me to the right. The sky opens its mouth and issues clouds that glow toxic red over the city and Joni Mitchell is on the radio singing a song I first heard in college: *What do I do here with this hunger . . .*

There were eight eager faces shining at me like moons, and I had all my favorite poets tucked under my arm—some dead, some alive, and me somewhere in between. I guessed that the girl wearing a pink sweater was from Sussex, England, just by her accent and the shock and pleasure on her face gave me a Henry Higgins-esque thrill. I let her talk too much, just to hear her voice. After class, the professor said it was the most he'd heard the girl say all semester.

Maybe it's the books sliding around on the seat next to me, or maybe it's those magazines that came in the mail reminding me I haven't seen London in two years. Anything seems possible on nights like this, as I drive steady into the wind, mentally emptying my bank account, devising an escape plan, wondering who will recognize my accent when I am far from home, reading poetry, more alive than dead.

MAGGIE KAZEL

FEAR OF THE LITANY

I remember thinking I teach every grade
every classroom that means eventually
I'm supposed to know every name.
How the hell do I do that?

I ask some other teachers.
No one has any tricks, they just say oh,
you'll get the hang of it, you will.

But that's because maybe I look like a teacher,
or a smart person, or adult enough to handle it.
I'm faking it, I can't do this, I've got them
all faked out.

Barely the end of September,
and Terry sees me kissing her
before I get out of the car.
Now I have to deal with this.
I may want to work here longer
than the end of the pay period.
Shit. So I go in, and I
wait till the end of the day.

Yeah, I saw you with her.
She's my lover.
Yeah, well I figured she wasn't just a good friend,
since my wife kisses me goodbye on the lips,
not my friends.
He was already being himself, Terry, teasing.
So I blurted it out, my fear of the litany
of names, my fear of faking
being a teacher and he said

124

Oh but you are.
You're right for this place and
you're right on schedule, breaking down.
You've got it, I've watched you with them.

What about technique, philosophy, content?
You might want to get your kiss
before the parking lot,
but even that . . . they trust you.
That's all it takes.

MAGGIE KAZEL

SAY GRACE, FIRST YEAR TEACHER

I don't know what started our talk,
me and my niece, nesting on my lap.
She asked me something and I said
maybe it's Indian.
My mind forgets the rest but holds
instant recall of her reply:
"They're dead."

I felt as though I was still on the plane,
approaching this niece,
my insides gripped by her words
feeling the pull of her gravity.
I knew that how I landed this thing
was everything—they're dead.
If they are dead, who am I?

I didn't tell all six of her years
about my job at the Indian school, or my driving
almost off the bridge after the interview so excited
by the children, the chance and then

how sick I was all that first month.
Dust, mold, rats, incessant cigarette smoke,
and culture shock combined
to rattle my lungs.
I scrubbed my basement storage/classroom and
then laid rat poison.
I cancelled everything else in my life,
even some friends,
after discovering I felt despondent or nauseous
when someone mentioned the latest computer
gadget or inseminating

method or problem
with men.

The dailyness of poverty.
Although I had problems with
incest scars, family drinking, insufferable work,
and suffering from the lack of work—
the poverty here I had never known.
And it was exhausting me.

A brunch group acquaintance said surely
there must be something
that is wonderful about working there—
their culture is so beautiful!
That was the other thing.
The exoticness weekenders could imagine escaped me.
I gave up casual weekend friend encounters after that.
I had spoken my truth, saying it's really hard,
I'm not sure what I do matters,
and then I tried to dance out some happy reason
for my work, some
logical explanation for my depression,
and then
I just quit talking
except to one friend who'd worked years in migrant fields,
and one who survived a small Iowa town,
alcoholic in recovery, lesbian in full bloom finally,
and my lover who put me to bed alone—the only
way I can sleep when I feel like,
I'd say I feel like I'm running a marathon,
and me, the one
who hates running.

What I steeled myself with
until that Thanksgiving
knowing violence and shame from childhood,
my lesbian sense of otherness

and my adopted/splintered heritage,
which shifts and tips and spreads
oblivious to anyone's edges.
These are the parts, shattered and within me:
illegitimate roots, adopted relation.
My blood runs invisible from and between
these inheritances.

This invisibility and the wisdom that springs
from it kept me running alongside
my students, faithful
and in case my own wisdom failed me I kept
Anzaldua, Gunn Allen, Brant—their soultalk,
their writings nearby.

Gracias, madres de alma, for my endurance.
This is how I got as far
as that moment: the end of first quarter,
greatly signified by my niece on my knee
and my Thanksgiving breaking
in her words, tainted
with the innocence of her years—

I endure to push the words out
They are not dead.
Push the air out of my crushed stomach
They are not dead.
Push my heart, pump the blood
into hand, into penwords for another teacher,
the one who took them to a museum.
They are alive,
and some of them
I have the honor of teaching
while they teach me
about everything I thought I knew.
Did I mention
they are not in the museum

and are as well as can be
expected in the city's ghetto?

This note to your teacher, niece,
no rage in my voice.
I pull out the pictures and she is delighted
when I tell her who drew them.
She's delighted they live and draw;
once dead, now drawing.

Next week in tobacco ceremony we share
our holiday stories of burnt turkey, deer that
came to hunters,
and I tell them about her,
about their deaths
in her mind, on her lips,
and I assure them I explained about their liveliness,
even though it is obvious to them
it is I who needs this telling,
this sort of thanksgiving.

I learn to say grace
by holding the mind of a child tenderly
as it lashes; writing to another teacher
the only words I can muster;
witnessing their breathing,
their ecstatic limbs, their unencompassed souls,
these Indian children, whose spirits are tested
on the toughest terrain.

And I move toward honor—to know the ways
spirit is beautiful in mere survival
while it testifies *all*
things are sacred,
all things
alive.

BONNIE S. KAPLAN

TIME FOR STUDY

Luis studied the dictionary while incarcerated,
read all the way through to S.

He loves vocabulary, asks me for two words a day.
I give him *inchoate* and *insalubrious*,
he knows both.

I need to be a little more sagacious,
give him words starting with T forward.

BONNIE S. KAPLAN

TALKING BAN

They have a male-female talking ban at the rehab.

Residents are not to engage in any discussion
with the opposite sex.
This conversation ban hinders intimate
relationships from forming within the community.

What about Terry who is transsexual?
I think everyone should be able
to talk to Terry.
The talking ban extends to my classroom,
I don't enforce it.
If Antonio wants to help Marquita
better understand the Barbarian takeover
of the Roman Empire,
then more power to that.

BONNIE S. KAPLAN

FRACTIONS

Heavier "cellie," call him Heavy-D,
gets the bottom bunk, *the denominator.*

The lighter guy is Numero Uno,
he gets the top bunk, *the numerator.*

Sometimes the two cellmates weigh
the same or the heavier guy
ends up on the top bunk.
This is called *improper.*

CHARLES JENSEN

FOR TEACHING ME TO TEACH

I'd like to thank the Academy for
expelling me. I fell to the ground
a mass of veins, plasma, membranes
nobody wanted. Then the chapter on
loneliness began with the phrase
He was a fish among birds. The book was
universally panned, nested with
disaffection in bookstore remainder bins.
The meanest critic called me out
like an umpire with an ingrown hair
you-know-where. He was vicious, viscous;
his lymph nodes twitched when he spoke.
I'd like to thank the Academy for
disavowing me. I roamed the desert
alone, just me and my gun, which
snickered when I pulled its trigger back,
shooting the arms off cacti too scared
to even move. I became an outlaw and so
wore a bandit scarf to conceal my smile,
which always betrayed my innermost desire.
I found a quarter on an empty highway,
then called someone who cared. They didn't
answer. I left a message on the machine,
mimicking Donald Duck. I imagined
that person's face when they heard it:
he might ask a friend, *Has Donald Duck
ever called you out by telephone?*
In retrospect I should have called for help.
I should have called the Academy to thank
them for teaching me to teach, thank them
for my hands inside my students' plaster, heating up,
burning their skin as I worked them out,

133

worked, worked them out of dust
and into the shape they're in now. All
it took was water. Things were simpler
then: we made what we wanted
and laughed like gods who didn't have to
wonder where their next meal was cooking.

CHARLES JENSEN

COMPLAINT OF THE COMPOSITION STUDENT

After reading the assigned passages, I was reminded how
all my life I never liked reading.
                     I never liked books,

turned up my nose at magazines, avoided all contact with
newsprint because more than reading
                     I, too, disliked

being covered with someone else's language.
If there were signs, I didn't decode
                     them. I simply

stopped, or crossed, or yielded if it pleased me.
When there were contracts, I
                     didn't sign. When it came

to typing, I played music instead, a fugue of syllables
I sang loudly and
                     without comprehension. When it came

time to declare myself, I stood silently by and let
others make their claims.
                     My head was full of themes

but none of them persuasive. I heard music then,
a cello mooing softly from the barn,
                     a violin

shooting an arrow of hornets from its bow,
chattering teeth in the clicking
                     of keyboards,

the moon's silent mouth, wide open,
writing nothing on its blank
                     page of night.

MARIA JASTRZĘBSKA

LESSON PLANS

Self-defence

When confronted with a knife
know a wall is just canvas for your leisurely
scrawl—girl loves girl, a maiden name—
think of a grey-skinned, posturing rhino
which scrapes the ground, bending saplings
into shapes—nothing is louder
than his voice inside your head.
His smallest finger is your only friend.

Wait years for the flicker of eyes
which tells you his grasp
has relaxed imperceptibly—
join Roller Derby or kickboxing classes,
take up the ukulele—don't hesitate.
Smell bad faith on his breath
do the very best
the very worst you can.

Assertiveness

Say: I can see you have a planet perched on your shoulder.
But the coffee is full of snow and hurts my teeth.
These shoes have pinched all my life.
Your thumb-prints were all over my body.
You keep looking straight through me.
Prostrate yourself—like a cloak on muddy ground—
so girls can walk over you to reach their dreams.
Return my calls, gaze.

Creative Writing

Don't be a starfish
leaving space is important
the reader will insert
her own meaning into each text in any case
don't make her do all the work.

Write more
or less.

BENJAMIN S. GROSSBERG

SECRET ADMIRER: AN ESSAY

1.

My first and only secret admirer sent me cards.
I was twenty-two, a new graduate student
teaching his first composition class
with a textbook and nervous energy enough,
usually, to make fifty minutes pass.

And here, just one month in, on my desk
in the shared grad-student office: a card
signed "your secret admirer." The card described
what I had worn that day and said I looked
"very nice," the writing tiny, precise, as polite

as a thank you note for an ugly sweater
written with mom hovering overhead.

2.

Some people teach by saying brilliant things.
I have learned to teach by asking questions—
because talking on with no response terrifies me.

But my favorite teachers have used the former method: going into their
classes was like strapping yourself into a cockpit, beside you the pilot
smoothly narrating a journey over New Zealand mountains. For years I
studied European history with the same professor. He was handsome, pale
blue eyes, maybe sixty, thin gray hair; his voice like a croon as he lectured
us through Byzantine centuries.

In retrospect, the line between admiration and desire feels less distinct.

3.

Why do people often end up contemptuous of the populations they serve?
Is there a way to avoid that?

4.

The next card showed up at my apartment—
no stamp, placed in the mailbox.

How did he know my address?
Was it a he?

Again, just a few words: *do you like me, too?*

Of course I did.
But who was it? The card was signed
by a number this time: 9. A clue.

5.

Teaching can arrange your personality around it. Maybe you start lecturing
to everyone. Or asking everyone follow-up questions, aiming to help
people articulate their full thought. Or—this is the one happening to me—
you become blandly supportive and encouraging of everything. We are, by
and large, impossible people to get along with.

6.

After that, cards arrived once every few weeks. I spent the term scanning
the faces of fellow grad students.

Urbane, troubled, they rested their cheeks
against their palms in class, nasally droned
lines of poems I'd never heard of, by authors
I'd never read. They had the mystique
of older siblings and characters out of 1960s

French cinema: black turtlenecks, long cigarettes—

It seemed impossible that one of them had sent the cards, but I wanted it to be one of them, any of them.

7.

Because I teach by asking questions, students may well confuse knowing me—liking me—with knowing and liking the function I perform. Liking being listened to, liking the feel of sustained attention. My face a beam that encircles, illuminates their subtleties, elicits, flatters. Flatters? Because students in our moment need it. Because without it, attention can glare, burn.

8.

The first time a student told me she had been molested, we were walking across campus, early autumn. I'd known her about six weeks.

Smiling up at me, she mentioned a poem
she had turned in, about a Christmas party
in which one of the guests, a parent's friend,
had crept upstairs to a child's room—
That one, she said, *the Christmas one, is about me.*

The first time a student told me he had HIV, he was pissed at me for being a hard ass about a deadline. He knew I was gay;

he laid his revelation down
like a full house: Aces over Kings.

9.

The number clues eventually formed a kind of sequence: 9-4-13-7-63. Something like that. I carried around a scratch pad.

10.

Sometimes you later read about them dying.

One had a blog where he recorded the progress
of his cancer. By the time he passed,
I hadn't seen him for a decade, and could not
reconcile the dignity of who he had become
with the kid he had been.

I suppose it shouldn't have taken sarcoma
to wake me to this possibility:
You were my student but now I feel humbled
by what you know, how you know it.

11.

So what can it mean when students say or feel that they like me? Though I
do try, also, to dress snazzily, and to make them laugh.

12.

The last card came—stamped this time, in the mail—
two days after my first term ended, December, 1993.
It was signed by one of my students.

He said he liked me because I addressed him
by name when I wrote comments on his essays.
No one in his country did that.

He said he was going back to Viet Nam now
and was sad he never got up the courage
to tell me in person.

He said he considered me his first American friend.

ELIZABETH GROSS

FIRST WORKSHOP
for Brad

Wearing their nervous systems on the outside
of their soul bodies—delicate, flashing
like bioluminescent jellyfish—is that terrible
to say? (see how I learn from them)—
they will try to take everything back
I mean with their eyes
wheeling around the circle like a lighthouse spot,
after they read out their made things
(we've talked about Greek roots).
They are just realizing the terror of making something true
by naming it, even if the wrong name is given,
even if nobody hears, even if you say
I have no idea where this came from.

GARTH GREENWELL

FACULTY MEETING WITH FLY

There I was, ready to die with boredom, and you—
you came to comfort me, sending through my arm

as you landed there a kind of pleasure that really
it's indecent to feel in public, among all these people

fascinated, apparently, taking such copious notes.
How can I care what they're saying when you ride,

balancing with your delicate wings, so brazen
the hairs of my arm, and in such an ecstasy!

No one before has traced precisely that path
along the thinner vein of my wrist, yet you take

such delight there, rubbing your hands together
or rearing back and prancing like a mare, while

beneath you subterranean my blood must roar
and thrum you like a lyre. Watching you polish

your black helmet already gleaming, sensing
already some scent in the stale air tempts you,

I shudder almost with a premonition of dismay—
then force myself to think of our differences of scale,

how for you already in these minutes we've lived
whole lifetimes together, a marvel of constancy,

really, and I forgive you, your brief form diving
now so gracefully away, air's blank currents

folding seamlessly behind you. And yet, abandoned
to this drone of serious voices, suffering

new extremes of detachment, how can I keep
from resenting what I've loved, when so inimitably

it flies off effortless to multiply its delights?

GARTH GREENWELL

AUTUMN STORM

Curled in the awkward chair, waiting nervous
for the doctor with his mask and his instruments
that always hurt, or threaten to hurt, however
genuine his promises of care, I think
what a curious exercise in civilization it is:
one animal letting another angle back its jaw,
clenching its teeth or not clenching them as
instructed. What a remarkable creature I am!
How obedient, how beautifully broken in!

Everything in the office is new, everything
so clean it hurts the eyes. A huge window
cut from the facing wall—more window
than wall—looks out over the highway named
for the president, long dead,
who built so many. Cars crawl past the strip mall,
the apartment complex where I live.
Saturday afternoon: Ann Arbor, Michigan:
late September, 2007. And even here,

in this place of ferocious diminishment—
what was pasture a year ago stripped now
for development, the ground just broken,
huge sheets of plastic flapping above
foundations that rise up like ruins in reverse—
even here, how much there is to see:
people about their business, curious narratives
on legs, their lives urgent or listless but
precious, sole possessions alienable

only once; in the median, serene, a goose tearing
at grass, alone, late for its migration; starlings

lining the wires that line the street, heads
back in their metallic songs; and, just
barely in the corner of the frame, a tree,
leaves already turning but its branches still full,
golden, in the slight wind each leaf singly
from the slim anchor of its stem shuttling
back and forth, shimmering, the whole of it

dazzling motion. It seems, from the distance,
as though along each limb there thrilled
a tongue of fire, burning
but burning without devouring; or like
the living bodies of bees, their forms commingled
in dance, with legs interlocked tumbling
in their drunkenness like tears of liquid gold—
as in the *Aeneid*, Book VII, the portent of a suitor
worthy gorgeous Lavinia, bringing greatness and Empire

and war without end. Why do I think, then,
not of a hero but of a boy, of the odd, intelligent boy,
hunched a full year in the back of my room,
latching his misery to me? One afternoon, late in the year,
when I was tired already, dejected, short-fused,
with terrible evident pleasure I shot out some snideness
so withering the class burst out in laughter
and a scattering of applause, all of them eager
for the punitive *we* in defiance of which

he strove in his solitary rage. I felt sick.
But what would it mean to make amends?
(Can this poem be amends?) He was who he was
already before, crooked already beyond
our power of making straight; he was like
a tree grown stunted in a stunted soil,
bound young with disfiguring bonds—
which is to say he grew a self like other selves,
the whole given shape to by the wounded part.

In the graying light less golden, the leaves
are whipped about now in a rising wind
bending ungracefully the branches. The goose
has flown off unseen somewhere, the starlings
dart from the autumn storm. Behind
the window streaked already with rain, I sit
in the warmth of the room and wait
for the dissolution of thought into salutary
pain, for the doctor who still hasn't come.

ARIELLE GREENBERG

SEVERAL FALSIFIED VIGNETTES ON CONSIDERING A CAREER IN ACADEMIA

I.   There was once a sharp-fisted, darkly-complected Ph.D. cowgirl
        sort of Djuna Barnesish figure only brusquer who does
        Renaissance and gender and on the weekends at her vacation
        house she moonlights (sunlights, really, during the day) as an
        orderly on the very serious fucked-up ward at the local asylum. She
        says this is her most meaningful work, and she says this even to
        colleagues she doesn't trust. You have to wonder why. You have to
        assume it's like an "I'm with the people" thing, and it seems pure
        and she is brutal in a noble way. You lack nobility and brutality
        but have petulance and a Valley Girl affectation in spades. You
        have to practice answering the phone in a way that sounds serious
        and professorial but still squeak "thanks!" as you get off. You had
        to record the outgoing message six times. You are sure she only
        had to do it once. Or maybe she's never bothered. She sort of
        shrugs off voicemail.

        A.   I am so fat it is like my stomach came from
                another body and got surgically attached. Or is
                that how everyone's looks?

II.   X likes to be challenged and yammers. It is simply that X has a lot
        to say. When X was young, X went to therapy because if X got mad
        at the parents, X would rock back and forth and stare at the walls
        and not speak a word. X was cured and now X speaks at every
        department meeting, even if X comes in late and has no idea
        where on the agenda they are. And X is not even tenure-track.

III.   The Professor looks to fashion as an emblematic, a post-ironic set
        of careful choices to confirm what? Abject horror at the self? Does
        the Professor even think of the body? The Professor seems to. The
        Professor goes to the school gym where the locker rooms are small
        and wet and have fleas. The Professor is muscle-bound. The
        students write in their assigned weekly journals, I saw my Professor
        in the gym. How brave of the Professor. It was weird but kind of

148

cool. The Professor—another Professor—lobbies a secret faculty committee for designated faculty gym hours to avoid this exact kind of unwanted encounter, but the main Professor likes to be with the students when working out. It verifies.

IV.   She's late for the secret committee meeting. At the door to the conference room, someone on a cell phone—staff? A graduate student? A guard? like a guard, but in a powder blue turtleneck and Caesar cut—asks if she is there for the right meeting, in the right room. She is, but once again, she look as if she's not. It's the patterned stockings. No one on the Task Force wears patterned stockings.

V.   The office door is kept open even not during office hours. This constitutes an "open door" policy which I like to extend. There is too much of a boundary already. I just tilt my computer screen away from the door.

      A.   By the end of the day, no matter how square-toed, your shoes pinch, and no matter how little you used chalk on the blackboard, your throat hurts. Thank god you have an MGM musical and some Reese's Peanut Butter Cups waiting at home.

VI.   My mentor, a retired diplomat adjuncting for his own amusement, thinks I might have a problem in class because I am "attractive."

      A.   I am too fat and the students know this.

      B.   It's just because I wear patterned stockings.

I know he means well but I am slightly politically outraged on principle. He likes me because I laugh at his jokes and he tells me so. It's like I am on a date with my grandfather. "No, you're doing fine," he tells me, and this only makes me worry. I don't want my students, who do not find me attractive, to know I am being observed by the diplomat, but they know. When he comes to class, they are no more or less sullen or agreeable than usual, but afterwards, they are mildly encouraging of me. "I couldn't write a paper about tripping on acid for *his* class," they say. I am grateful and stern, as is appropriate.

149

ARIELLE GREENBERG

BRING A STUDENT DOWN

T=Tell

There are three or four stations available.
One or two circuits may be busy.
And there's no insurance,
there's no insurance,
at the bottom of the staircase
there is no floor at all,

The X.X.X. Suicide
Prevention and Response
Protocol

just a drop.
Drop down.
It's a smoky situation with no insurance.
Also, she did it, and he did it,
and the teacher said,
You have to respect that decision.
It's good to be in control.
It's good to feel

Assess the immediate risk

if the door is hot; you can
use the window. The office comes
with a half-hour prevention presentation
but when we call the number the line is busy
or no one is there. There's help
and then there's up.
Get back to what life?

Remember—
You are not alone!

There have to be other services in place:
food. Love.
A work schedule on a dry erase grid.
A place to go home to.

As poets, we are most proud of our
accomplished suicide alumni.

ARIELLE GREENBERG

WHAT I DO: AN ESSAY

I poetry. I make it (often sideways leaning over into the passenger's seat of the car on the back of a Wild Oats receipt or a syllabus), I talk about it to students, I rarely but joyfully talk about it with friend-poets, I read it for journals I edit, I read it for class, I read students', I order theirs and my own into manuscripts, I memorize and forget most of it.

We were very tired, we were very merry.

Sometimes I tire of it and wish I made beautiful chairs or dresses or posters. I dislike how it likes itself, how its practitioners get slavish, are photographed doing it in creaky barns with big mugs of tea atop their gorgeous desks, how precious and rarified it all is. How it seems to require pounds of tea. As an antidote to this I put in tutus and bars of soap and television stars and my sex drive and mouth-plaque. This is not always a cure. I am still a precious animal by
nature.

I want to be at least as alive as the vulgar.

I do not do anything else as well or as happily or as easily as I do this. I am a hedonist in this one thing, my "calling." (Precious!)

I also mama. I'm doing it right now, in fact, invisibly, semi-visibly, under my shirt, forming this very week, nostril holes and toenails in the one-to-come. At the same time (magic!), I help my daughter choose a raincoat from the L.L. Bean catalog. I get out some banilla yogurt (precious!) from the fridge and adorn it with a tiny spoon.

How do you like your blue-eyed boy now, Mr. Death?

These precious things actually muddy up a poem, because these things of home are still not the tea and the barn and the original Rauschenberg over the beautiful desk piled with books and papers. As Rachel says, to poem and mama you must shut a door very hard.

It was not night for all the bells put out their tongues for noon.

I keep the door open. Mama's in the office. Mama at her school. I keep the door closed.

Don't protect me from my life, I say. I have to be in it. The mud is what I'm after. In poem-making. In my mama house, I'd like most of all a mudroom, a place where I can leave my boots but still track in the dirt all over me.

DANIEL GONZALES

(UNTITLED)

Preschool

I see the way he moves
The voice, the fey octaves
The wiggle of hips
The playful manner in which he teases the other boys
They know he is different
I try to be kind to him, smile and tell him to settle down
Treat him like all the others
Some of the boys are already growing aware
We live in a world where masculinity is taught early
They know he does not belong
Some of the boys try to push him on the playground
I am the first to blow the whistle
He cries and I tell him to dry his eyes
I don't want them to see
His mother always makes him the perfect bologna sandwich with the
crusts cut off
The girls let him join in their circle, they play tea party
And talk about the boys they will marry when they grow up
The boy's father always looks embarrassed when he picks up his son
He tells him not to move like that
Not to talk like that, not to be like that
It makes me want to cry
Because I used to be that boy.

Elementary School

A teacher's lounge is no different
Than a lunchroom cafeteria
There are cliques and groups and gossip
And rumors, those eyes, the staring

153

The insinuations, the way they get quiet
Whenever I come in the room
The way the football coach laughs
Whenever he sees me pull out my lunch
Organic, gluten-free
Girl food, he calls it
"Why aren't you married?" they ask
"How old are you?"
"How long have you been single?"
Is there something so strange about a thirty-two-year-old man
Who teaches English and isn't married
The first thing women do when they see me
Is look for a ring and then they smile
And show me their cleavage
I try to be polite
Sometimes they persist and I have to tell them
"No thank you, my husband is at home"
"Oh," they say with that face
The embarrassment enough for both of us
But I don't have a partner, I don't have a husband
I have a cat named Charlie and a ton of student loan debt
My kids are already learning how to be men
They say the word "gay" as if it is an insult
I try to correct them, this has gained their suspicion
Soon they are talking about me behind my back
I see notes passed and crude caricatures
They are studying my movements
Anything deemed less than manly
There is a boy named Tommy
He calls me a faggot to my face
I take him to the principal
And he awaits his fate
His father is a construction worker
Reddened hands and broken skin
His mother is all smiles and blank stares
They apologize and he is given detention
They stare at me, they study me

As if they KNOW and are afraid to say anything
I can imagine the lecture they give him
And tell him to just keep it to himself
They don't correct the behavior
They just teach him how to hide it better
Soon the lunch room is abuzz with the story
They ask me endless questions
They are afraid to ask
The coach won't even look at me now
"What did he call you?" Miss Pilner, the math teacher asks
"Fag," I say, the entire room grows silent
"But it doesn't bother me," I say, "I am gay"
One woman smiles, a few people leave the room
One of the older women winces
And I walk out of the lounge, smiling to myself.

High School

"He should not be allowed to teach our children,"
The first woman says
"It is not natural," the second woman says
"AN ABOMINATION TO GOD!" the man says
They are the types who have never left this town
In their entire lives
I refuse to back down.

I hold the book firmly in my hand
Thomas Mann's *Death in Venice*
One of the boys complained to his parents
That he had to read a book about a gay person
We started having open discussions in class
This is a small town, news travels fast
Suddenly I was promoting an agenda
I was infecting the minds of youth
My car tires were flattened

A meeting is called

The school board is there and about twenty angry Christians
And another dozen outside with signs
I am ready to give up
Hate is a wall that only reflects back on itself
I am blinded by dogma
The head of the board slams her gavel, asks for order
The gallery is restless
I think of my warm bed and a bath

Then I see them
My students leading a small parade
A tiny rebellion of six
Creeping inside, holding signs and taking their place in the back
One of them asks if they can speak
It is Samantha Ryerson, one of my best students
They have come to defend me
Tears are running down my cheeks
As I hear her voice
The words are a blur
All that matters is they came
The council hears their voices
The words of young adults with open minds
Their target audience
Not these poorly lead alliances of rage
They want to see me fired
I am ready to resign
The woman lays down the gavel and takes a vote
My students watch me with anticipation
Samantha's eyes meet mine
7-4, I get to stay
The book however is nixed from the agenda
I thank the board
Then my students
Yet going home I wonder if anything was won
I feel as lonely as Thomas Mann.

PIUS GONE

INQUISITION

My sophomores are curious creatures
barbed with the confidence of adolescence
grown from a history of being told
they have no dumb questions
only questions deserving of answers
questions to which I am dumb,
that the tie-tight Mr. façade
answers well enough, like:

I. "Is that a mood ring?"

of straight moods and gay moods
and other moods yet undefined and roaming
a spectrum of *ROY G BIV* moods
Oh Nick, if the wood in this band would say anything what would it say?

II. "Are you married?"

Whom are you asking?
Do you mean the minimum wage clerics
who took a couple hundred cash
for pose for the photograph flash and a congratulatory certificate, a paper
I taped to the refrigerator like some finger-painted masterpiece
from a child I cannot adopt
until the irony ate him up and he told me
to take it down?
or
the State

of benefits   of denial
of taxes   of anger
of visitations   of fear
?

III.   "I saw you at the Street Fair on Saturday."

An observation, true, not a question
but like most observations this one had a fishing line
—small, invisible string—tied to its hind leg.
A string that came with a question
clutched in the hand of Theseus
Theseus; these fifty pair of eyes
staring the question out of the air
With whom?
With whom?

My family
My sister
my mother
my father
my   cousin/friend/old college roommate.

I rarely feel glad he hates holding hands in public spaces.
I rarely feel glad   in public spaces.

A professor once quipped to me
that the question mark reminded him of a scythe.
I, the visual learner
have yet to unsee that
a quest inhabits each question,
of search and discovery and
I have yet to find the time
or the shame large enough
to fit the honest conversation
that my students, my Mr. Teacher,
and whatever's left of my Self
can't have
—yet.

PIUS GONE

POEM WRITTEN MINUTES BEFORE SCHOOL STARTED, SEPTEMBER 2011

Humility is
hearing the click-click-click
of your student walking down the hall
to your class.

Humility is
hearing the click-click-click
of your student wearing leopard print pumps.

Humility is
watching your student share the delight he has
in his new shoes with his friends.

Humility is
a reminder that change, like water,
seeks out the path of least resistance.

D. GILSON

MARTY IS A LESSON IN GRAMMAR

I don't know why I think of him
on this cold March Tuesday, but from
the front of the classroom, it's clear
I have forgotten my brother's
lesson in grammar, when he taught
me how to conjugate dirty
Spanish: *correrse*, to ejaculate.
A student asks, "what is future
perfect tense?" Add this to the list
of things forgotten. Such as:
I have forgotten my brother.
I have forgotten my brother
took me fishing. And all the cakes
we baked for Mother's birthday,
all the camp outs and spelunking.
Joan says, "when you kill yourself,
you kill every memory." Perhaps.
I have forgotten my brother's
birthday, or I would have, had it
not been the day before my own.
Marty's candles always come first.
I have forgotten my brother
and his tense: not future perfect.
He will have left thirteen years back.
So maybe he is future perfect.
I will have forgotten my brother
and how he died at thirty and
Mother cried *baby, oh, baby!*
In this way Mother is future
perfect. She has not forgotten him,
my brother, and she cannot finish
her sentence, so cradles him close:
baby, oh, baby, oh my baby, oh.

D. GILSON

SONNET BEFORE INTRODUCTION TO SHAKESPEARE

In the parking lot of the community college
where I teach, a young woman walks by
a Chevy Camaro where a young man sits
listening to Eminem and smoking weed.

Though I am not old, I am too old for this
I think, walking into the gray cinderblock
building. I sit by a window in the faculty
lounge and check my e-mail. Outside

the man is talking to the woman through
the lowered glass. He turns up the bass
as Eminem sings *I'm not afraid, I'm not
afraid, to take a chance, to take a chance,*

and she kisses him through the car window
as I wish for them, love, despite what I know.

REBECCA LYNNE FULLAN

HOW TO BE A TEACHER

First,
despair of what you know.
It will not be enough.
It is not the right kind.
You are as unprepared
as you fear.

Let the things you know
fall out of your hands
and shatter on the floor.
They will not fall
in neat pieces
but blow away instantly
in dust.

This dust will coat your hands,
your students' faces. It will get
into your lungs and make you cough.
It will get into your eyes, where it sparkles
and refracts.

Bring stories in your open hands.
There will be questions like, what
is a devil? How many quotes
are we required to use? Do you want
a revolution? Would you, personally, go
to the site of one? When is that essay due,
again, and what is it about?

When one of them tells you he cannot write,
ask him to draw. And when he draws a fish,
look at the fish. And when he writes about the fish,

take what you know about him now, as mysterious
as what you did not know before, and hold it.

Love your students. Surprise and disappoint
them. They will do the same for you.
They will write you on New Year's Eve.
One will send a picture of her bandaged head.
One will send an essay for revision.
One will ask you, do you understand how I feel?

Take what you know now and hold it close.
Make it into pottery, something beautiful.
Next time you begin a class, hold it in your hands
on the very first day, when you wish
you were a plumber or a politician or
anything but this—and let it drop.
And so begin.

REBECCA LYNNE FULLAN

THE PERSONAL ESSAY FOR COLLEGE ADMISSIONS

The boy's casual loopings
of language and his mid-sentence
twistings pull me into the curve
of his meaning, blistery
and ungrammatical,
walls wet with whispers.

Everybody-knows-them secrets
laid out in stylings, lurid and florid,
and devil's-tail-curlicue
nowhere prose, and there behind a door—
his true thing, invisible to the
bearer, with blind baby eyes
and a nose needing warming,
and a wicked rhino horn.

He'll tell me again how time left him,
how his country language parents left him
in the care of giants without
mercy, in the care of mercy without
mercy, in the careless wild intervals,
extraordinarily bold
in their shaftless, shiftless
carving of the life that came before.

He has learned.
He is stronger.
It is resolved.

I walk behind, dogging his steps,

untangling and reweaving like
a revisionist spider. I stand
beside him and believe the fiction—
together we believe the fiction
not that it is resolved, for we each
feel the slice of edges against testing hands,
but that it can be resolved,
that resolution is there, around that corner,
under that sentence, waiting, with the tingle
of our tongues under ice cream,
in the shiny gold bauble of a word
we learned in perfect isolation
from its use.

REBECCA LYNNE FULLAN

THE RESEARCH CLASS

Some of us expect bombs,
bullets, punches. The end
of current safety, forever razor-edged.

Some of us expect these things,
and some of us throw them,
and some of us dodge them.

Some of us raise our faces up with questioning.
Some of us keep our heads down,
our shoulders hunched in jackets,

lest our faces betray us. Our faces
always betray us—our feelings and our
colors on display, for others to

determine the meanings of, who
are often unkind. Who are often
brutal, and we do not expect

less. Most of us, it turns out,
are feeling that violence is
imminent, hanging low

in the air like thunder. None of us knows
how to prepare. This is a class
on research, and we are talking

about the future; we are telling
each others' fears and reading them
like palms, feverish attention

to the lines, my thumb pressing
against your skin. I pace up
and down and say things that invite

my own intense biting criticism,
things about vulnerability and
courage, and I sit on the table

and I say, tell me, tell me what you hope
for, and tell me what you are going to
do.

Superheroes, justice against
corrupt cops, a decent job and the
apocalypse, organ donation

and recycling and our personal
moral codes and keeping our
heads down, minding our own

business and reaching out our
hands and our veins and our
kidneys, from time to time,

when the moment is right.
Some of us believe in these things,
and some of us write poems about them—

not just me. This is the research class
and this is what we have learned. Every
time is a late time and every generation

trembles and vibrates: fear and possibility.
The things we expect
are coming.

JIM ELLEDGE

OFFICE HOURS

Shhhhhhhh. (Lust saunters in, wearing jeans bleached
at the crotch, and plops down beside the desk, legs

spread wide, thighs flexing, relaxing, flexing . . .
Lust licks his lips. Relaxes. Flexes. Lust leans

in, a question hovering in the bright air
between them, part riddle, all tease like a shiny

red apple hard in a hand, juicy in a mouth,
dripping down a chin. What is it that Lust asks,

his hand inside his Dago-T, rubbing his pecs,
tweaking his left nipple until it's paying attention—

something he didn't bother to do all semester? *How long
does it have to be?* Maybe that's it. Or, *How long*

before it's due? That must be it, but out in the hall,
waiting for our next class, we can only guess

although we've heard Lust's whiskey voice that's
so '40s noir and got lost in his eyes, now busy

rummaging the professor's lap who adjusts himself,
pulls out his grade book, and uncaps his Bic.)

MEG DAY

TO MY STUDENT, WHO ASKED, "SINCE WHEN DOES A BUNCH OF NORMAL PEOPLE STANDING AROUND ACTUALLY CHANGE ANYTHING?"

I say, *You're right.* When she spoke during my junior high trip to San Francisco,
she was specific about the seat, how she refused to stand; fifth row on the right,

bus #2857, lucky window spot freed up when another passenger moved on back
as asked. Eighteen blocks from that auditorium, the 'Loin's tender hold of Gene

Compton's Cafeteria now sways gentle-hipped in its newest incarnation, a leaning
SRO, all kinds of folks still crowding the curb with cigarettes & strings of single

syllables for those whose stares linger too long. It's true, I think; they are rarely
just standing around. The few who sat drinking Woolworth's coffee in Greensboro,

the four million who walked out after Kent State, the solid week of fists in the air
at Gallaudet—the burning scarecrow, the news stations that invested, suddenly,

in closed captioning. How did it happen that you have the entire world at your
fingertips & know nothing of the lineage on which Wall Street tents are pitched?

How exactly do you think change comes about? We stand. Like the two hundred
thousand that remained in place for seventeen minutes of one man's dream, like

the planted feet of every human chain outside of every Planned Parenthood, like
the rows upon rows of bodies stomping dust in Arizona, a solid wall between

the flashing lights & the random bend of the border. Like today in Oakland,
when a young black man stretched out his hand to a row of white riot shields,

every gun tipped with petals. There is a reason we stand in ovation. There is
a reason we stand for something. There is a reason we stand up, do not

stand back, stand in solidarity & do not cross the picket line.
Young man, you have no idea what's coming.

THERESA DAVIS

SIMON SAYS

Don't you remember that time in your life?
When you were all arms and awkward intentions.
Aggression wrapped in a barbed-wire heart.
When you were minx and sass, teenybopper,
borderline juvenile delinquent. When the closest
you wanted to be to other people was way
the heck over there.

When your body turned battlefield.
Bones aching, tonal war of vocal cords.
When you didn't know where you fit,
but you wanted to so badly, you buried
whatever you thought could be held against you
in the backyard next to GI Joe and Barbie.

It is here that I need you remember who you used to be
so you can fully understand and appreciate what happens next.

For the sixth grade science teacher, who after a female
in his class asked to be excused twice during his lesson,
felt it was appropriate to announce to her classmates
that it must be her time of the month.

Before that moment, science was her favorite subject.
She was going to cure cancer. Return renegade memories
to Alzheimer's patients. She can't stand science now,
and what I think she means is that she can't stand you.
But the cause and effect of your forked tongue
has left her casualty, period.

For the seventh grade English teacher, who in her infinite
wisdom saw fit to suspend a thirteen-year-old boy
for three days because the wind blew at the wrong time

and things became erect.

Now she doesn't understand why he won't talk to her.
Why he is so cautious in her classroom-turned-minefield.
He is silent because that is the one thing he can control,
and since she seems determined to punish him for the things
he can't, why would he give her more ammunition?
He is cautious because she has turned enemy camp.

Now she wants to scream zero tolerance
like that's synonymous to hijack your own common sense.
I have zero-tolerance policy in my classroom.
Talk during one of my tests, watch me hand-grenade
launch your efforts into the nearest spherical filing receptacle.
But in 2009, when Simon stood erect, slammed his pencil
on his desk in the middle of my math test and said

Ms. Theresa,
I'm just saying, if Freddie Mercury were alive today
we would not be at war with Iraq!

I think three things simultaneously.
First I think he knows who Freddie Mercury is!
Second I think his parents are awesome because
he know who Freddie Mercury is!
Third I think he could be right and who am I
to punish him for his insight?

When teaching our children
we have to remember that we were once one of them,
and shaming them about the bodies they are trying to invade
the voices they are struggling to own, will not win us their trust
it will only render us untrustworthy.

So, educators, choose your battles
quiet your voices sometimes so you can
better hear theirs.

Do this, and I guarantee
our young people, they will ROCK YOU!!

PENELOPE DANE

LOW LEVEL

On the day the queer student
panel came to speak, I worried
about the reaction. It was the Deep
South. It was English class, but

most of section 56 focused, except
the Christian frat boy in the front row
who radiated fear as he scratched
letters into a crossword puzzle.

When he finished, he erased
so hard his desk squeaked.
I imagined his pencil emitted ionizing rays
which refracted off us all.

The other students
and the four panelists
kept on, twisting their fingers.
They answered questions

about god, dating, their families.
He began the crossword puzzle again,
his pencil fired out
letter after letter.

I regret that I waited

until after class to confront
him about the crossword puzzle.
I was too afraid of
detonating in front of them:

then all the students would figure me out.

Years ago, I studied gamma radiation
and I learned that low exposures
over time can damage more

than one mean dose
because our bodies don't
even notice the small cell mutations
from low levels and

the cells never think to try
to fix themselves because
they don't know anything
is wrong.

LOUIE CREW

IT'S NEARING EXAM TIME

I can tell because my first heckler in Newark
called to tell my answering machine,
"You still owe me for that blow job that I gave you
on Broad Street, and if you don't pay up,
I'm going to claw your balls off, you hear?!"

What's disappointing is that the caller
is one of my favorite students, a female
who has done quite well in the course.

She does not know that I have a new gadget
that tells me the number of those who call.
Nor has she read my gay beads yet.

Well, at last I am a citizen of New Jersey.

Some people mark their establishment
when they register to vote,
others when they change their insurance address,
others when they get their first pay check,
others when they join a new parish . . .

I know that I have arrived
when the first heterosexual nuisance call arrives.
At one time I had recorded enough of this rare species
to make a long-playing record.

LOUIE CREW

LIVING HERE

I deliberately drove home the shortest way
not to avoid the Latino ghetto
and the Christopher Columbus Homes,
long ago evacuated and now "occupied"
by crack heads, prostitutes, and the homeless.

"Since I have moved to Newark, I will live here,"
I insisted to myself, going and coming to work.
Most here don't have the option of safer,
longer routes. Why should I?

Late-afternoon traffic kept a snail's pace
in the thick heat of July.

Ahead, several teenagers played street ball,
I bemoaned impatiently, and then I panicked
as I saw three of them, shirtless, tough,
leave the game and head directly to my car.

Have you ever tried to lock your doors
and close your windows without letting folks
around you observe your fear?

I scratched my head to disguise my elbow action.
My right hand crossed my lap to do the window switch.
All the while I looked down so they could not
read the fear in my eyes, praying they would pass me by.

They didn't. One tapped heavily on the window
I pissed a bit before I saw a familiar face
smiling through the glass. He still tapped.

"Hi, Doc," he said. "I want you to meet my friends,
Carlos and Juan. Fellows, this is the teacher
I told you about."

Less than two hours before,
this "thug" was the best prepared in my class.

I was the only menace here. I have only myself to fear.

EC CRANDALL & JASON ZUZGA

HOMOSEXUALS AND SCENERY

"Scenery in the film shows just how Homosexuals can take a beautiful day and end it in tragedy."

When I read this sentence in your introduction, I am attracted to the unintentional truth of your observation. You make me want to think more about homosexuals and scenery and question queer assumptions about beauty and tragedy.

Beauty rising again? I cede the floor and disappear into the wall.

In my Indiana elementary school, David McIntyre, the literature teacher, was a tall, flaming intellectual who wore ugly sweaters and slick pants with pleats. I have fond memories of his fussy brown penny loafers with the tassels. Gayle Gunns, the gym teacher, was a butch dyke with a flat top who, on occasion, would pull out our lucky loose teeth during cool down. Years later, she would swim the English Channel. Like most of my friends, I was pulled into the orbits of these two rival planets, only for me this uncharted cosmos seemed composed of my own dueling interiors. Before I graduated to middle school, David and Gayle were married, a meeting of the mind and body so to speak. A crushing disappointment for us all—a mystery even—although we didn't know the word "gay" or how to process what felt off beam about this marriage. We only knew it didn't make sense, that the wedding had taken their magic away. At least they kept their jobs, if that was their panic. They divorced years later, their 50s scam a provisional farce.

Lucky loose teeth. The things that come out of your mouth! You think everyone's a homosexual.

Meanwhile, in New Jersey, Mrs. Della Williams has been teaching for decades and faces another deskload of beauties and the odd asymmetric. Not her choice, but the youthful skin and mom-washed clothes drive her to her bottle of scotch in the drawer. Or so we said. In my presentation on Faulkner, she permitted me with a frown and raspy *whatever* to build a fire in the center of the room with four thumb-wicked citronella candles in tin buckets. Dump leaves all around the room. Tape opaque trashbags to the windows. Spray all the students with pine scent deep woods Off.

That tree at the end in motion with squirrels.

I want to make one thing clear: you have to be weird to teach. If you have a talent for any of the following, it will certainly help: costume design, particle physics, hairdressing, social work, party planning, computer programming, food preparation. You'll have to learn to set the scene.

Clear, uncluttered communication.

Lug logs into a circle around the fire, drape sheets over the piled desks in corners, play a loud cassette called "Southern Swamp" and the croakings and the bubblings soaked the volume of the room, all dark, classmates' faces flickering as one by one. They read aloud passages from Faulkner's "The Bear" passing flashlight and book around the circle of us perched on the logs, legs touching, the words incense the hair on arms read along with the whirr of the insects calling to mate. She made sure we taped opaque the window in the door.

Passing the flashlight, I rubbed on a leg.

My mentors who are queer did not have queer mentors. Not in the strictest sense. It's a fragmented legacy at best; however, one that dates back to the ancients. To teach is queerly optimistic.

Aren't you my mentor, mentor? I had none before or so I thought until.

I hated the phantasmagoric preciousness of *The Scarlet Letter*. Mrs. Williams suggested I read the bitchy satire I wrote to the whole class. Woman has a piece of toast ribboned to her cheek with a burnt letter that ever shifts, births an oyster. When a snicker for Whitman *faggot he was a faggot* crunched in the back of the class and began to flame up, she rose to

178

her full height, grizzly bear, whiskey-blotch stain on her old sheer blouse, no bra, she roared. Bear mother, guard of we, she growled a roar of fire and quashed that devil shard of intimidation into dust spiraling up marvel at the ferocity of Whitman.

Faggot flame guard. Everywhere, mentors, not even hidden in the walls.

"Due to the fact that homosexuality was contagious and anyone could get it, I believe that's the reason why the film was titled *Beware Boys!* Homosexuality is conformity because it's not ideal, it only would hurt the population and is socially rejected." I wonder where I exist in your daily experience, or even if I'm anywhere near the periphery when you type this sentence. For instance, is there a space for me in your daily mind life where I slump at a desk in a classroom? Do you know I'm there, even if I don't participate? Have you recognized me? I am in your same cave, with the same lights and shadows.

Near the periphery, stoking the classroom, poking the marionetteers.

When I get a paper arguing Nan Goldin should be killed so she can go right to hell where she belongs because her photographs promote homosexuality, I tell this student one-on-one that I am gay, and that I remain unconvinced by her argument. I don't protest her point but try to treat the essay with clenched respect, and I try to bring our two lives into a hybrid scene in which Goldin brings us both a bracing sight. How could I open Goldin up to this kid from a small town in Arizona, all that raw undetermined space?

Who am I to imagine myself the arbiter of queer?

Is the act of listening really that queer? Is it all an act? We often teach students to hear strange, new sounds in ways that will become comfortable. But to stay in the space of strange and let them hold ground with their arms out may be just as liberating. To let the sound of difference proceed. Is it for us to say what shaking is? Ugh, when I have feelings of giving up, I stick to teaching *taste*.

Fine, then stay uncomfortable.

It would have been better, she said, if we had built a real fire. And I come out now as a matter of course before every class, bury it in with some other topic. As a student lifts up his Arizona t-shirt to show his Arizona tanned, tight stomach to me, his gay prof, as he asks me if I might raise a grade, I laugh a Della laugh at him.

The grade remained eternal C but, beauty, yes—hot as he was young.

WRITE ABOUT THIS DO NOT STOP WRITING UNTIL THE FLOWER FALLS. Time going backwards, lines read backwards, queering a reading of any old sentence can be old news. But old news can be a mentor. Mary Poppins brings John and Mary and the baby to a candy store where the proprietress breaks off her fingers to treat them, sweet knuckle suck cinnamon suck, finger pointing peppermint suck and chocolate swirl.

What if I suck as a teacher?

When the student writes in her course evaluation, "I think I fell in love with her," I question to what extent this happens to straight teachers. I lament, "Has this student learned anything about provocative performance in this class?" Learning is an erotic space for some of us, but thrust upon a queer adult love object this proclamation bespeaks Tolerance! Diversity! Self-exploration! The deliverables of the neoliberal university. The first crush I ever had on a teacher was a straight English professor whose name I can no longer remember. I had been queer for four years, having momentarily blossomed into a harmless militant lesbian. He dressed horribly and was kind, easy. Perhaps we who teach texts are always transmitting, *question this*, *question everything*, somehow from the signals in our bodies.

Question this question.

I am excited to attend my student's production of *Last Summer at Bluefish Cove*. I have helped her with her panic attacks, and her strong opinions have become crucial to the second half of the semester. I invite one of her classmates, a troubled, talented gay boy who has followed me from class to class for two years, to come along with me. When "straight" Stacy climbs onto the stage wearing butch flannel and huge black fishing boots, I beam with eerie pride and can't help but wonder if she had unknowingly been my understudy for the past four months.

A comforting hum.

The long fingernails of the librarian scrape as he turns the page to read John Bellairs's *The Clock in the Walls* illustrated by Edward Gorey. I thrill at my disgust for his mellifluous voice, the thrill of disgust at the strange, a burning knife of a thrill turned within. Like: fear. Like: things inside of things. Who was this strange man?

Maybe he was just a goth librarian.

Identify yourself.

XXX XOXO

MICHAEL G. CORNELIUS

MY COLLEAGUES TALK OF TITS

My colleagues talk of tits.
They laugh in that
conspiratorial way
I think all straight men do
when I am around.
One girl—just turned
twenty—they call her
hover-tits, and they
laugh again. I take
a bite of my egg salad
sandwich and
frown. This is
wrong, and I say so.
They look at me as
I eat lunch with them,
and I am mindful that my
invitation can be revoked
at their whim.
Silence falls over us,
and I realize, as I so
often do, that I do not belong.

They are men.
I am not.
This is the implication
of their stillness.
Who am I to—?
They are good men.
That is what their silence
haughtily says.
Married. Children.
They only talk. Think.

Desire in an errant, almost
casual way. Their
minds meander, like the
knights in the stories I
teach in my 3:00 class.
This is what it means
to be in the locker room.
This is what it means
to be at their table.

I am a teacher. I
want to yell. They are
my students. I do
not speak of them like
this. And thus I wallow
in my own self-
righteousness.

Then I think of
tousled hair brown eyes
knit cap molded athletic
legs in active bottoms from
TJ Maxx in the fourth row,
and I blush.

CHARLOTTE CLUTTERBUCK

FORCED INSPIRATION

The sawfinch reiterates
his rasping notes
teacher, teacher
with all the characteristics
(though unmusical)
of nuptial music.

The muscles that assist
the action in ordinary
tranquil inspiration
are the intercostals
and the levatores costarum
(the muscles which immediately
invest in the chest).

Levitating on the highwire
wobbling from rope to rope
the teacher, not wanting to be shamed
in front of her pupils
hurtles down the flying fox.
In all expulsive acts
the diaphragm is called into action
to give additional power.

Some bodies are not visible
to the unaided eyes
because our pupils
are not large enough
to grasp sufficient light.
We must therefore borrow
assistance from some device
which shall have an equivalent effect

184

to the enlargement of the pupil
beyond the limits
that nature has actually intended.

I am not supposing
that her machinery has broken down
(that slowly and with hesitation
the clang of her anvils dies away
while all stand dismayed)—
of course that sometimes happens
at sea, as do calamities
of a far more tragic nature.
What she wants is merely
something like a funnel
which shall transform
a large beam of rays
into a small one.

CHARLOTTE CLUTTERBUCK

OFF THE MAP

Put on your spectacles,
measure the shortest-distance-A-to-B red lines,
set out on a quest
for your planned destination—
a professorship, perhaps,
teaching what you learned
on the pilgrimage to Canterbury, or Truth
or the Celestial City.

Later, you find the map in the glove-box
tattered, faded, broken in the folds,
arterial roads severed,
the red bleeding off the edges of fragments
and the square Windsor-to-Armidale
gone missing.

Unemployed, take your grandson
to Questacon, buy
a spy mirror. Hard to control.
Bending what's round corners,
the prism refracts
not the paintings you aim at
but odd recesses of roof, light fixtures,
a fragment of a sculpture by Brancusi,
the edge of a bird in flight, wingless,
a flash of water reflecting
beams, girders, louvers, sky.

Meandering here, picnic in a lay-by
with students whose roads have been potholed,
bridges broken by accident or tumours,
who write with a gaiety of unchosen images,
and you find here something
you'd have missed on marked roads.

CHARLOTTE CLUTTERBUCK

No

No singing in class
no coming last in the race
no missing the bus
no whingeing on your first day
in a new country
when your sea-legs wobble
on the trek to the sandhills
no smudging your book
no you can't win the essay prize
no you can't be form captain
no you're too messy
no she won't read your novel
written in the bus with pencil on a scribble pad
no you can't stop going to mass
no you wouldn't be a good diplomat
no you can't write a thesis
about Grammar AND God
AND Poetry AND your own
spiritual journey, no you can't
be broad AND shallow
no your poem isn't good enough
no we won't pay for your poem

no I haven't enough time
no I have to hang out the washing
no I haven't been to Africa
no I haven't worked with the starving
no I can't write *Paradise Lost*
no the language has changed
and I can't write harbinger
without sounding pretentious
no because I'm a woman
no because I have to visit my grandchildren
no because I have to teach Chinese students to write their PhDs
no because I have to visit Centrelink

187

no because my ambition is just
attachment to worldly success
no because the ego is an illusion
no because I have to buy bacon for dinner.

JAMES CIHLAR

MAN PROOF

Color is in the air between us. Call it Spiritus Mundi
or the collective unconscious, it is the teal and salmon
of the upholstered headboard, the ivory of the sheers
around the four-poster bed, the Windsor blue
and Persian cream of my dressing gown's floral print.

I've been neither one thing nor another. The world you see
is not the world I live in. No silver balloon floating on a string
behind the white stripes of Venetian blinds.
For me it is primary red, an ache of the in-step,
Franchot Tone sweating under the lights.

I'm nothing but a nothing. Let's mock the barbarians in the ring.
No matter if they look like John Garfield and William Holden,
W.B. Yeats and C.G. Jung. Maybe someday I'll see my face up there.
Forgiveness is okay. I want the story to end before it becomes a story.
Hello, Mother. I'll wager I look great in a blonde wig.

You talk and I'll listen. Franchot Tone folds like a bad hand.
Tell the story backward and the balloon recedes behind a door.
My memory is your memory, my dreams are your dreams.
If I am standing on a cliff, you are on the other side. Goodbye, Mother.
It was a good fight, and the better man won. Anyone got a ducat?

RENNY CHRISTOPHER

SCHOOL IS

where kids are taught to say their abcs
and memorize the pluses and take aways
the capitals of all the states
the dates of all the wars.

It's where kids are taught to sit
in neatly ordered rows
taught to color inside the lines
taught to raise their hands for permission.

School is held in buildings
that look a lot like prisons
where children learn not to be
too creative, not to be too different
or unusual, learn to be good, obedient
citizens of an unjust world.

RENNY CHRISTOPHER

THE WEEK AFTER SEPTEMBER 11, 2001

As I walk from the parking lot across the campus,
I approach two students sitting on the sidewalk,
sketch pads on their knees, intent on their pencils.
A third stands in the shade to the left of the walk,
and a fourth out on the grass in the sun, and I realize
this is an art class, out sketching the trees and the fountain.
As I pass behind the two seated students I peek
over their shoulders and see the heavy, awkward pencil lines
with which they've rendered the trees. A beginning class, it must be,
and I feel peaceful and right, thinking this is the proper business
of the university, of humanity—to try and draw the trees and the water,
to try to transform one kind of beauty into another,
the best kind of alchemy we know.

But as I walk on, the moment of silence and peace passes as the voice
from the radio I've just turned off echoes back in my head.
Right now the US Fleet is converging at a staging point, ready
to perform a different sort of transformation, of buildings into rubble,
of peace into chaos, of life into death, of power into supremacy,
ready to bomb a poor and devastated country that already has
half-a-million disabled orphans because the tyrants who rule there
despite rebellion and resistance won't hand over a lone man
who stands accused of crimes against a nation possessed of military
might and moral blindness.

While the students are sketching trees our nation is going to war
again, going to kill again. If I could bring peace by sketching trees
and water, by writing poems, by burning myself on the steps
of the Lincoln Memorial, I would do it. But I do not know what alchemy
transforms madmen to peacemakers—not their madmen, and not ours.

RENNY CHRISTOPHER

SIXTIES GENERATION

Once when all of us
were young
(were we ever so young?)
explosions and napalm and teargas
and fear
came to us direct
or indirect
up close and personal
or on TV
you could get your leg torn off
you could get your moral universe
shattered.

Now
gray and paunchy
we fight
a war of words.
We sit still
in academic halls
speak into microphones
talk and talk
take the old positions
over and over
now all we can lose
is an argument
the stakes much lower
but we act as if
they were still high.

The man at the podium says
students
must make

not only their future
but also their own past.
For us
that past remains
incompletely made
unresolved
grasping us still
making us.

JAMES BURFORD

DANGEROUS THOUGHTS OF A QUEER/TRANS AWARENESS EDUCATOR

Sometimes when I educate
I am called to trawl through the gutters
Of my mind
I want to
Dredge up muck and gunk
Present rude words
In bad taste   (bet they'd taste good though)

I think strategically about what to wear
find myself taking off rings, broadening my smile
My voice comes out breathier,
I almost always wear boots

I contemplate deploying rudeness
Wonder about the potential of liberating bitter feelings—
Education as not filling the cup with sunshine and promises
But spilling it
Staining the carpet with some home truths

Sometimes I think of
reconfiguring queer/trans awareness education
As SM
Puncturing the façade
Revealing the kink, the roleplay
And being real (playful) with power

I guess I am still figuring out
How far I can push things before they fall over   (maybe they should)
How generous to be,
And when to make them squirm

JAMES BURFORD

MS. ARETHA BROWN

Ms. Aretha Brown,
Betcha didn't know
I called you that,
didja?   I think your assigned name was Dorothy.

It was the jazz in your voice,
that low growl,
and that fact you let me write poems in maths class
that gave me cause to honour you with the title
Aretha.

Someone said you were a dyke,
doesn't matter to me
if you were, weren't,
or will be.

I recall my delight in your
stiff, robotic body,
flat chest,   (maybe you were binding?)
square hands,
and country-butch clothes,
(you *always* dressed like you were showing ponies at the A&P.)

One event that returns to me is when
mean Melissa barked
about the polish on my nails, or powder on my nose,
I stood up   and screamed,
stopped the class for minutes
for the first time,   and
allowed all of the breath in my body to rush out at her at once.

You said nothing.   That was enough.

If I'd been a womyn, I'da been like you.
Staunch,
               tired
I wrote you letters
punctuated with xoxxxxxxooooooxxxxxxxxxxxxxx
and the lyricz of my favourite songz.
I scented them with my deodorant.
They *were* love letters.

Ms. Aretha Brown,
for many, the gifts you gave remain unopened
but I carry mine in/on me.
You can hear it   in my own voice when I teach
and read it   between the lines around my eyes.

ELIZABETH BRADFIELD

DISTANCE EDUCATION

In Unalakleet and Gambell, my students,
teachers' aides who need this class
to keep their jobs, learn this week that they must care

about the semicolon. More
than their properly punctuated sentences,
I want to read what stories

they tell themselves to make
it matter, this stuff that someone who can legislate it
thinks they should find important.

I don't know when the murre eggs
are ready for harvest or when
walrus meat tastes best.

Hard to care about the split
infinitive when ice storms,
when past dues, when shore erosion.

I assign homework they don't do
because they had to take kids
away from their fathers or because

cloudberries ripened in the bog.
I look at my spreadsheet of work done
and points assigned. The icon for its program
is green as new shoots of pushki. I fail them.

ELIZABETH BOSKEY

THE IVORY TOWER

When I was packing my boxes to leave the academy
Books neatly stacked
Diplomas wrapped carefully in brown paper
Odd collection of tea mugs swaddled in the sweaters I wore
In the winter when the heat didn't work
And frost formed on the insides
Of the dusty panes that barely brought light into my office
I heard a knock on the door.

The student who followed the hollow sound
And stepped across the grey tinged tiles to my desk
Was there to chastise me.
"How can you leave?"
"Who will speak for us after you go?"
"I feel invisible and unwanted."
"The other teachers will never understand."

I couldn't disagree.
The academy, as I knew it.
Was partial to bias.
Where hate was absent, ignorance reigned.
Another teacher once brought in a lesbian
For show and tell.
I felt invisible myself.

I wanted to tell her that she was lucky
She would only be there for two years.
While I wanted to protect her
Stand for her,
Speak for all those young people
Whose own voices were silent
The thought of being trapped forever

Prisoner in the ivory tower
Was killing me.

Climbing down the braided rope of words
I had created in my bid for freedom
I chastised myself for abandoning
The queer students
The different students
All the young people who felt safe with me
When it seemed like the rest of the world was against them.

I wished I could bring them with me.

TOBY BIELAWSKI

THE SEDUCTION OF COMPARISON

The white birds—gulls, I guess—circling over the park
Are so small, so far off
I could've thought they were trash, pieces of paper
Caught in a breezy vortex.
In class, my students revise their papers
Agonizing over the thesis
No, I tell them, it is not enough
To say this is similar to that, but different,
Such and such is different from thus-and-so
Still with many similarities though.
A statement like that has no point, I tell them;
They look aghast. *Anything* is like and unlike
Something else—you have to push farther. Try.
One girl seems about to cry.

What I tell them is true: the papers
Will not do, even though driving to work
Just this morning, I saw buffalo-shaped trees
Grazing dry grass, and thought how the freeway
Rode the hills like a rollercoaster track.
How will we know, Kevin asks,
When a statement has a point? Wanting to reply,
Instead I am looking past Roneisha's cornrowed head
Out the window at the vineyards behind campus
Woven tightly up the slope.

TOBY BIELAWSKI

THE HOMEWORK IS LEAVING HOME

Who uses these words?
Pairs of eyes glare at the book,
At me, all snark.

The words glare back
At the eyes, at me,
At their own pages.

No one, I say, no one
In the home you left
This morning. Between

Lands, languageless, my
Classroom is a customs house
What are you bringing in?

They stare at the book,
At me, unaware how to
Declare vocabulary.

OLIVER BENDORF

TEACHING TIME

To teach my students
the subjectivity of time,
I instructed them to rest
their heads on the tables
and quietly raise a hand
when they felt two minutes
had elapsed. Around
eighty seconds in, the first
brazen hand lifted up.
Then more trickled in.
By three minutes, all students
had one hand in the air
except Greg. Greg's shaggy
hair rested motionless
on his elbows. I waited.
At five minutes, it struck me
he might be asleep. But
to stop the game now
would be to fail them
at my own experiment
of demonstrating
time's capricious ways,
how the same moment
can either dilate or contract
depending on who
you ask. Six minutes.
I thought about the drive
home after my Nana
had finally died, how
the usual forty-minute
commute felt at least
six times that long. And

I thought about
the weekend my partner
and I had jetted down
to Key West (seven minutes),
how four days felt like
just as many seconds,
even though—I'm told—
island time moves slower.
Island time. I thought
about that webcomic
that laments how you can't
use Halberstam's theory
of queer time as an excuse
for lateness.
I can't remember
at this point whether
any of the other students
lifted their heads
to see what in the hell
was taking this exercise
so long. I was too
busy staring at Greg,
wondering what kind of
counting system was going
on inside his head, or—
more likely—whether he
had in fact fallen asleep.
I remember when I first learned
that dreams only last
a couple minutes, even if
they seem to span days.
I can never tell when
a finger has reached
my elbow. At minute
twelve, Wendy
rose quietly and left
to use the restroom.

As she walked out
I caught her eye. I used
to do this thing
in elementary school
where I'd try to catch
a classmate's eye
long enough to
tell them something
in my head, like: *Please
invite me to your birthday.*
If Greg would just look
up for three seconds,
I could ask him with my
eyes: are you in there?
Do you dream in color?
How long has it felt like
since your last haircut?
At fifteen minutes,
Wendy returns. And
just then, I hear Greg
whisper, "a hundred
twenty" and then slowly,
methodically, lift a hand
above his head.

LIZ AHL

EAVESDROPPING ON THE ENVIRONMENTAL BIOLOGISTS

One table over at the university snack bar,
they speak of flow augmentation,
freshwater applications, wastewater treatment,
nitrates, and cloudy waters; of plant infestations
in a particularly loved cove and of all the magic
conjured to battle the invasion.
They lean in, huddling over the map
as if it were a rich green pool
of something worth studying.

At my table, I hover over
a small stack of student poems,
each one a creature I'm trying to understand.
Already, they have started to infest me,
an alphabet of tentacles, a cloud of spores,
but I will them into symbiosis.

It's Valentine's Day,
a good day for all creature-lovers.
I want to send a valentine verse
expressing this sentiment
over to the biologists, who seem
so trustworthy and devoted to the lake—

but I am shy
and they are busy
solving lake problems.

I return to the words of my students,
keep still as possible and let them crawl
across my face, which is maybe too close,
maybe not close enough.

LIZ AHL

ELECTRIC HOMEWORK

"I'll send you an electric copy of my homework."
– a student

He'd make a great young Frankenstein, wild-haired,
lab-coated, surrounded by the noisy, elaborate apparatus
he'll use to animate his short-story scenes
into lurching, misunderstood life.

Or a Ben Franklin, flying his key-kite
into the ominous clouds, going upside-down fishing
for the spark he suspects is swimming around up there.

I'm thrilled at the prospect
of what might genuinely shock me
in that way language has—a little *bzzt*
to remind you you're alive in this world.

From now on, it's mandatory—electric homework.
No more limp and quiet pages, passively
nodding in the general direction
of language's hot wires. Instead, dear students:

Hook your homework up to your car battery
and give it a jump, so its engine roars to life
and I have to leap out of the way.

Rub it vigorously across the carpet
or a red balloon so that when I touch your words
they explode under my fingertips.

Plug it into so many extension cords
you start a subtext fire.

Take it to the emergency room
and get House to lay on the defibrillator paddles.
Build a hydroelectric dam to harness your hot tears
so they don't get hung up in empty cliché.
Send all your stumbling stitched up creatures
and crackling science fair transgressions
my way, and let's see where the currents take us.

blank
page

CONTRIBUTOR
BIOGRAPHIES

JASON ZUZGA's poems and essays have been published in journals such as *Chainlinks, LIT, VOLT, SPORK, jubilat, The Yale Review, Drunken Boat* and *EOAGH*. He is a recipient of poetry fellowships from the James Merrill House and the Fine Arts Work Center in Provincetown and completed an MFA in poetry and nonfiction at the University of Arizona. Currently, he is the nonfiction editor of *FENCE* and a graduate student in the English PhD program at the University of Pennsylvania focusing on postwar ecology and documentary media.

GERARD WOZEK currently teaches Writing and the Humanities at Robert Morris University in Chicago. His first book of poems, *Dervish,* won the Gival Press Poetry Award. His most recent book of short travel stories, *Postcards from Heartthrob Town,* was released by Haworth Press.

GREGORY WOODS is Professor of Gay and Lesbian Studies at Nottingham Trent University, United Kingdom. He is the author of *Articulate Flesh: Male Homo-eroticism and Modern Poetry* (1987) and *A History of Gay Literature* (1998), both from Yale University Press. His poetry collections, of which the latest is *An Ordinary Dog* (2011), are published by Carcanet Press.

NICHOLAS WONG is the author of *Cities of Sameness* (Desperanto, 2012). His poems are forthcoming in *American Letters & Commentary, Gargoyle, Harpur Palate, Interim, The Jabberwock Review, The Journal, Natural Bridge, The Pinch* and *upstreet*. He is the recipient of Global Fellowship Award at Arizona State University's Desert Nights Rising Stars Writer's Conference in 2012 and a winner of *Hawai'i Review*'s Ian Macmillan Writing Contest (Poetry) in 2012. He is a poetry editor of *Mead: Magazine of Literature and Libations* and reads poetry for *Drunken Boat*. He has recently been nominated for a Pushcart.

CYRIL WONG's last poetry publication was *Satori Blues* (Softblow Press, 2011). His poems have appeared in *Atlanta Review* and *Poetry International* and have been anthologized in *Language for a New Century* (W.W. Norton,

2008) and *Chinese Erotic Poems* (Everyman's Library, 2007). He lives in Singapore with his partner and best friend.

RIVER WOLTON grew up in London and now lives in Derbyshire's Peak District. She is a facilitator and performer and was Derbyshire Poet Laureate 2007-9. She won first prize in the *Chroma* International Queer Poetry Competition of 2008. Her collection *Leap* is published by Smith/Doorstop.

SCOTT WIGGERMAN is the author of two books of poetry, *Presence* and *Vegetables and Other Relationships*. Recent poems have appeared in *Spillway*, *Assaracus*, *Naugatuck River Review*, *OVS*, *Chelsea Station*, *Southwestern American Literature*, *Contemporary Sonnet* and *Hobble Creek Review*, which nominated "The Egret Sonnet" for a Pushcart. A frequent workshop instructor, he is also an editor for Dos Gatos Press, publisher of the annual *Texas Poetry Calendar*, now in its fifteenth year, and the recent collection of poetry exercises, *Wingbeats: Exercises and Practice in Poetry* [swig.tripod.com]

DANIEL NATHAN TERRY is the author of *Capturing the Dead* (NFSPS, 2008), which won The Stevens Prize, and a chapbook, *Days of Dark Miracles* (Seven Kitchens Press, 2011). His second full-length book, *Waxwings*, was published Lethe Press in July of 2012. His poetry has appeared in many journals and anthologies, including *New South*, *Poet Lore*, *Assaracus* and *Collective Brightness*. He teaches at the University of North Carolina Wilmington.

YERMIYAHU AHRON TAUB is the author of three volumes of poetry, *Uncle Feygele* (Plain View Press, 2011), *What Stillness Illuminated/Vos shtilkayt hot baloykhtn* (Parlor Press, 2008; Free Verse Editions series) and *The Insatiable Psalm* (Wind River Press, 2005). He lives in Washington, DC. [www.yataub.net]

GABRIEL SYLVIAN researches Korean same-sex literary history at Seoul National University and actively promotes the translation of same-sex themed works by Korean writers into other languages. Translations include Shin Kyung-Sook's *The Strawberry Field*, which appeared in *Azalea: Journal of Korean Literature & Culture*, and, still in-progress, *Warning at the Station: the complete works of Gi Hyeong-Do*.

MOLLY SUTTON KIEFER's chapbook *The Recent History of Middle Sand Lake* won the 2010 Astounding Beauty Ruffian Press Poetry Award. Her work has appeared in *Harpur Palate, Berkeley Poetry Review, you are here, Gulf Stream, Cold Mountain Review, Wicked Alice* and *Permafrost*, among others. She received her MFA from the University of Minnesota, serves as poetry editor to *Midway Journal* and curates *Balancing the Tide: Motherhood and the Arts | An Interview Project*. She currently lives in Red Wing with her husband and daughter, where she is at work on a manuscript on (in)fertility. [mollysuttonkiefer.com]

SOPHIA STARMACK received an MA in French and Francophone Literature from Bryn Mawr College and is currently pursuing an MFA in poetry from Sarah Lawrence College. She has taught in high schools, colleges and community centers in the United States, France and Turkey. She currently lives in Brooklyn.

RUTH L. SCHWARTZ has published five collections of poetry, including *Edgewater*, a 2001 National Poetry Series winner, and a memoir. She is the recipient of sixteen national writing awards, including fellowships from the National Endowment for the Arts, the Ohio Arts Council and the Astraea Foundation, and teaches in the Ashland University low-residency MFA Program. A lifelong explorer of consciousness and healing, Ruth holds a PhD in Transpersonal Psychology; she offers private workshops, mentorships, and HeartMind Integration sessions worldwide. Ruth's physical home is in Oakland, California. [www.evolutionarysupport.com]

RUTH ROUFF is a freelance educational writer who lives in southern New Jersey, near Philadelphia. Her essays and poetry have been published in various literary magazines including *Exquisite Corpse, SLAB* and *Philadelphia Poets*.

JOSEPH ROSS is a poet and writer in Washington, DC, whose poems appear in many journals and anthologies including *Poetic Voices Without Borders 1* and *2, Drumvoices Revue, Poet Lore, Beltway Poetry Quarterly* and *Full Moon on K Street*. In 2007, he co-edited *Cut Loose the Body: An Anthology of Poems on Torture* and Fernando Botero's *Abu Ghraib*. He has been nominated for a Pushcart Prize. [www.JosephRoss.net]

RON RIEKKI wrote *U.P.: a novel* (Ghost Road Press), *Your Map is Wrong: a Collection of Plays Set in Michigan's Upper Peninsula* and *Dandelion Cottage, A Play* (Center for U.P. Studies), *Leave Me Alone I'm Bleeding, She Took God: a memoir in 44 poems* and *Poems about Love, Death and Heavy Metal* (Gypsy Daughter), and he has books upcoming with Wayne State University Press and Michigan State University Press. For drama, he also wrote *Dandelion Cottage, A Play* (Lake Superior Theatre) and *All Saints' Day, AKA 44 poems about Jeffrey Jones* (Ruckus Theater). He wishes whoever is reading this much peace and happiness and even more peace.

ROMA RAYE is a teacher, parent, partner and burly butch spoken word poet who lives in a little house in the suburbs of Seattle. Focusing on the powers of poetry, protest and possibility, Roma, as a Radical Teacher, brings the mic to the classroom and the students to the stage. When Roma isn't chasing adolescent minds around an overcrowded and undersupplied English classroom in Federal Way, Washington (Go Gators!), you can find her reading comic books and daydreaming of Disneyland.

DOUGLAS RAY is author of *He Will Laugh* (Lethe Press, 2012). A former Lambda Literary Foundation Poetry Fellow, he received his BA summa cum laude in classics and English and MFA in poetry from The University of Mississippi. He teaches literature and writing at Indian Springs School, an independent boarding and day school in Birmingham, Alabama.

AMANDA POWELL's poems are in journals and anthologies including *Agni, Borderlands, CAB/NET, Canary, Hunger Mountain, Mudfish, Northwest Review, Partisan Review, Ploughshares, Poetry Northwest, Women's Review of Books, Sinister Wisdom, Zoland, From Here We Speak: Oregon Poetry* (Oregon State University Press) and *My Lover Is a Woman* (Ballantine). Her translations of Spanish and Latin American poetry include *Sor Juana Inés de la Cruz, The Answer/ La Respuesta* (Feminist Press, 2009). Awards for poetry and translation include Massachusetts Poetry Foundation, Oregon Arts Commission, Oregon Humanities Center and National Endowment for the Humanities. She teaches Spanish and Latin American literature and translation at the University of Oregon.

KENNETH POBO won the 2011 poetry chapbook contest from *Qarrtsiluni* for *Ice And Gaywings*. Also published in 2011, from Deadly Chaps, was his collection of microfiction called *Tiny Torn Maps*.

NINA PICK is a queer poet, counselor and teacher from Massachusetts. She taught college writing classes while she was a graduate student at University of California Berkeley, from which she holds a MFA in Comparative Literature. She currently works at the Hawthorne Valley School, where she has taught high school classes in Literature and Health/Wellness and is completing an internship in school counseling as part of a second Masters program in Counseling Psychology.

DONALD PERRYMAN is a retired high school teacher of the gifted and an amateur poet living north of Atlanta, Georgia. He is currently assembling a first book of poems, written over a period of many decades.

SHANNON PARKER teaches information literacy and technology skills at a suburban middle school. She and her girlfriend live in St. Louis, Missouri, with their dog, Riley.

ERIN NORTHERN is the host and co-organizer of OUTSpoken, Albuquerque's first Queer Poetry Slam and Open Mic. She enjoys teaching first grade with Albuquerque Public Schools and is a member of the 2011 ABQSlamsPoetry Team. She was a featured poet at the 2011 Atlanta Queer Literary Festival and was Albuquerque's representative for the 2009 Women of the World Poetry Slam. Erin's poems have appeared in *Adobe Walls II, III, & IV: An Anthology of New Mexico Poetry, The Pedestal Magazine* and *Feminism NOW*. In the community, Erin facilitates ongoing safe-space workshops to empower queer identified youth.

BONNIE J. MORRIS is a lesbian-identified professor of women's history, teaching at both Georgetown and George Washington University. She also grades Advanced Placement United States History exams for the College Board. She's the author of eight books, three of which were finalists for the Lambda Literary Award (*Eden Built By Eves, Girl Reel, Revenge of the Women's Studies Professor*); her latest book is *Women's History for Beginners*. Here in DC she's also on the board of Mothertongue, the spoken-word stage for women poets; she was recently profiled on C-SPAN Book TV and elected Professor of the Year at George Washington University. Out and proud since age 18- (1980!).

CARIDAD MORO has appeared in numerous journals and anthologies such as *Here Come the Brides! Love and Marriage, Lesbian Style, Just Like a Girl: A Manifesta, The Lavendar Review, Calyx, The Comstock Review, MiPOesias* and others. Her chapbook, *Visionware,* is available from Finishing Line Press as part of their celebrated *New Women's Voices Series.* She resides in Miami with her nine-year-old son and her partner, fellow poet, Stacie M. Kiner.

LISA L. MOORE's poems have appeared in *Experiments in a Jazz Aesthetic, Sinister Wisdom, Broadsided* and *Lavender Review.* Her poem "Anthropomorphic Harp" won the Art/Lines Juried Competition for Ekphrastic Poetry, Museum of Fine Arts-Houston. She is Professor of English and Women's and Gender Studies at The University of Texas at Austin.

STEPHEN S. MILLS has an MFA from Florida State University. His poems have appeared in *The Gay and Lesbian Review, PANK, The New York Quarterly, The Antioch Review, The Los Angeles Review, Knockout, Ganymede, Poetic Voices Without Borders 2, Assaracus, New Mexico Poetry Review, Mary* and others. He is also the winner of the 2008 Gival Press Oscar Wilde Poetry Award. His first book, *He Do the Gay Man in Different Voices,* is available from Sibling Rivalry Press. [www.stephensmills.com]

LUCIEN DARJEUN MEADOWS is a being concerned with Be-ing. He began writing as a child among the mountains of Monongalia County, West Virginia. For Lucien, poetry is an alchemical process informed by the confluence of myth and modernity, the narration of self and the construction of gender identity. His poetry has appeared in journals such as *Appalachian Heritage, Battered Suitcase,* and *Quarterly West.* Lucien is an MFA candidate at Southern Illinois University in Carbondale, where he lives with his cosmic cohort, radiant muse, divine spark!—and a plastic cat named Euripides.

PABLO MIGUEL MARTÍNEZ's work has appeared in numerous publications, including *Americas Review, Borderlands: Texas Poetry Review, BorderSenses, Comstock Review, Harpur Palate, Inkwell, La Voz de Esperanza, New Millennium Writings, North American Review* and the *San Antonio Express-News.* He has been a frequent contributor to the *San Antonio Current.* Martínez is the recipient of the Robert LB Tobin Award for

Artistic Excellence, the Oscar Wilde Award and the Chicano/Latino Literary Prize. His literary work has received support from the Alfredo Cisneros Del Moral Foundation and the Artist Foundation of San Antonio. Currently he teaches English at Lone Star College in Houston.

TERRY MARTIN has published over 250 poems, essays and articles and has edited both journals and anthologies. Her first book of poems, *Wishboats*, won the Judges' Choice Award at Bumbershoot Book Fair in 2000. Her most recent book of poetry, *The Secret Language of Women*, was published by Blue Begonia Press in 2006. She teaches English at Central Washington University and was honored as a United States Professor of the Year, a national teaching award given by the CASE/Carnegie Foundation to recognize extraordinary commitment and contribution to undergraduate education. She lives with her partner, Jane, in Yakima, Washington, The Fruit Bowl of the Nation.

JEFF MANN's books include three collections of poetry, *Bones Washed with Wine, On the Tongue* and *Ash: Poems from Norse Mythology*; two books of personal essays, *Edge: Travels of an Appalachian Leather Bear* and *Binding the God: Ursine Essays from the Mountain South*; two novellas, *Devoured*, included in *Masters of Midnight: Erotic Tales of the Vampire* and *Camp Allegheny*, included in *History's Passion: Stories of Sex Before Stonewall*; two novels, *Fog: A Novel of Desire and Reprisal*, winner of the Pauline Réage Novel Award, and *Purgatory: A Novel of the Civil War*; a collection of poetry and memoir, *Loving Mountains, Loving Men*; and a volume of short fiction, *A History of Barbed Wire*, winner of a Lambda Literary Award. He teaches creative writing at Virginia Tech in Blacksburg, Virginia.

RALPH MALACHOWSKI lives and works in New Jersey. He received his MA in English Literature in 2002. A number of his poems have been published in print and online. He works for the State of New Jersey and is an adjunct professor at William Paterson University.

ED MADDEN is the author of *Prodigal: Variations*, a collection of poetry. His first book of poetry, *Signals*, won the South Carolina Poetry Book Prize. His work also appears in *Best New Poets 2007* and *The Book of Irish American Poetry from the Eighteenth Century to the Present*. Madden is an associate professor of English at the University of South Carolina where he teaches Irish literature, creative writing and gender studies.

KERRY MacNEIL is a teacher and writer who lives and works in northern Manhattan. Her work has been published in *Girls*, *The Journal of Lesbian Studies*, *Beyond Survival* and *The Q Review*.

HADAR MA'AYAN is a public middle school teacher, educational researcher and writer. Her recently published book *Reading Girls: Adolescent Lives and Literacies* is available from Teachers College Press (2012).

RAYMOND LUCZAK is the author and editor of 15 books, including *How to Kill Poetry* (Sibling Rivalry Press, 2013) and *Among the Leaves: Queer Male Poets on the Midwestern Experience* (Squares & Rebels, 2012). His other poetry collections are *Road Work Ahead* (Sibling Rivalry Press, 2011), *Mute* (A Midsummer Night's Press, 2010), *This Way to the Acorns* (Handtype Press, 2002) and *St. Michael's Fall* (Deaf Life Press, 1996). His novel *Men with Their Hands* (Queer Mojo, 2009) won first place in the Project: QueerLit 2006 Contest. A playwright and filmmaker, he is the fiction editor of *Jonathan*. He lives in Minneapolis, Minnesota. [www.raymondluczak.com]

NATHAN ALLING LONG's work appears in seven anthologies and over thirty journals, including *Tin House*, *Natural Bridge*, *The Sun*, *Marco Polo* and *Indiana Review*. For several years he served as the prose editor of *RFD* and currently is on the board of *Interalia*, an international online journal of Queer Studies. His work has won a Truman Capote Fellowship, a Mellon Foundation Fellowship and a Pushcart nomination. He lives in Philadelphia and teaches at Richard Stockton College of New Jersey.

TIMOTHY LIU is the author of eight books of poems, most recently *Bending the Mind Around the Dream's Blown Fuse*. Translated into ten languages, his work is archived in the Berg Collection at the New York Public Library. A contributor to many anthologies, including *Collective Brightness*, Liu lives with his husband in Manhattan.

G. M. LANG teaches high school English and journalism at Kingswood in Wolfeboro, New Hampshire, and dabbles in verse and the odd play or short story. He is the 2011 NEATE Poet of the Year, and in 2010 he was awarded the Marlon Fitzwater medallion for his work in teaching journalism. He is an active board member for the Poetry Society of New Hampshire and an active coach for Poetry Out Loud. His work has appeared in various poetry journals, in the 2008 and 2010 editions of *The*

Poets' Guide to New Hampshire and in his own slim volume, *No Match for a Scarecrow*. He is currently editing the Poetry Society's anthology of poems about aging and memory, tentatively titled *You Must Remember This*.

SARAH-JEAN KRAHN holds an MA in Cultural Studies and Critical Theory from McMaster University. She has "instructed" in Cultural Studies, English and Humanities. Currently she lives in Alberta, Canada, with two cats, a dog and a human.

MIODRAG KOJADINOVIC is a Canadian-Serbian poet, prose writer, journalist, translator, interpreter and photographer. He has postgraduate degrees from Serbia, Holland and Hungary, has done research in Norway and taught at universities/colleges in Mainland China, Serbia and Macau. His writing has been published in English, Serbian, Dutch, Russian, Hungarian, Slovene and Chinese in Canada, Serbia, the United States, France, Russia, China, England, Holland, Slovenia, India, Croatia, Australia and Montenegro. He has also appeared in three documentaries (of which one was about himself as a globetrotter seeking a place under the Sun).

JEE LEONG KOH is the author of three books of poems, the most recent being *Seven Studies for a Self Portrait* (Bench Press). Born in Singapore, he now lives and teaches in New York City and blogs at *Song of a Reformed Headhunter*.

GEORGE KLAWITTER taught literature at St. Edward's University in Austin, Texas, for eighteen years before moving back to Indiana in the summer of 2012. *Country Matters*, his first book of poetry, appeared in 2001, and his book *Let Orpheus Take Your Hand* won the Gival Press Poetry Prize in 2002. *His Noble Numbers*, his most recent book of poetry, appeared in 2011.

CAMDEN KIMURA is a writer, reader and tea drinker. She lives in California with a parrot cichlid named Ke$ha and a pregnant cat named Franklin.

COLLIN KELLEY is the author of the novels *Conquering Venus* and *Remain In Light*, which was a 2012 finalist for the Townsend Prize for Fiction, and the short story collection *Kiss Shot*. His poetry collections include *Better To Travel*, *Slow To Burn*, *After the Poison* and the recently published *Render*. A Georgia Author of the Year Award winner, Kelley's poetry, essays, interviews and reviews have been published in magazines and journals around the world. [www.collinkelley.com]

MAGGIE KAZEL is a writer, mom and lesbian-in-full-bloom-finally living along the shore of Lake Superior in Wisconsin. Maggie has taught in a K-12 school, colleges, halfway houses and jails. For her, teaching is heaven and hell, and writing, the elixir that makes all things bearable or better. Her work has been published in *Sinister Wisdom*, *Untangling the Voices*, *the Evergreen Chronicles* and most recently in the *Migrations' Anthology* by Wildwood River Press.

BONNIE S. KAPLAN has worked full-time with adults on parole for over 12 years as a teacher in the California Department of Corrections and Rehabilitation (CDCR). As a correctional educator in the Preventing Parolee Crime Program, she has seen the power of poetry to heal the soul. She teaches basic writing and math to paroled adults, and she often reads her students' poetry and reads poetry to them. She was accepted into the Squaw Valley Poetry Workshops in 2011.

CHARLES JENSEN is the author of four chapbooks and a collection of poems called *The First Risk*. His work has appeared in *Field*, *New England Review* and *Prairie Schooner*.

MARIA JASTRZĘBSKA was born in Warsaw, Poland, and came to the United Kingdom as a child. She co-founded Queer Writing South and co-edited their anthology *Whoosh!* (Pighog Press) and *Different and Beautiful - Writing by lesbian, gay, bisexual and transgender young people* (Allsorts Youth Project). Her own work is frequently anthologised, recently in *Collective Brightness* (Sibling Rivalry Press) and *This Line Is Not For Turning Contemporary British Prose Poetry* (Cinnnamon Press). Her most recent collection is *Everyday Angels* (Waterloo Press), and a new book is forthcoming later this year. She co-translated Iztok Osojnik's *Elsewhere* (Pighog). Her play *Dementia Diaries* toured nationally.

BENJAMIN S. GROSSBERG is an associate professor of English at The University of Hartford, where he teaches creative writing. His books are *Sweet Core Orchard* (University of Tampa, 2009), winner of the 2008 Tampa Review Prize and a Lambda Literary Award, and *Underwater Lengths in a Single Breath* (Ashland Poetry Press, 2007). A chapbook, *The Auctioneer Bangs his Gavel*, was published by Kent State in 2006. His poems have recently appeared in *New England Review, North American Review* and the 2011 edition of the *Best American Poetry* anthology.

ELIZABETH GROSS left her heart in New Orleans and part of her spine in Prague. The rest of her lives in Brooklyn for the moment. Her poems have appeared in the *New Orleans Review, The Prague Revue, Versal, Vlak* and *Why I Am Not A Painter*. She teaches writing and literature at Hunter College and also works as a literacy warrior for a full time remedial program out at Kingsborough Community College.

GARTH GREENWELL has published poems in *Yale Review, Boston Review, Salmagundi* and many other journals. His work has received the Grolier Prize, the Rella Lossy Award and a prize from the Dorothy Sargent Rosenberg Foundation. His first book, *Mitko*, won the 2010 Miami University Press Novella Prize. He lives in Sofia, Bulgaria, and teaches high school English at the American College of Sofia.

ARIELLE GREENBERG is co-author, with Rachel Zucker, of *Home/Birth: A Poemic* and author of *My Kafka Century, Given* and several chapbooks. Ugly Duckling Presse will republish her chapbook *Shake Her* in 2012. She is co-editor of three anthologies, most recently *Gurlesque* with Lara Glenum, and is the founder-moderator of the *poet-moms* listserv. She left a tenured position in poetry at Columbia College Chicago in 2011 to move with her family to a small town in rural Maine.

DANIEL GONZALES is a 34-year-old writer living in Seattle, Washington. He is a licensed therapist and school counselor. He is currently editing an anthology of fiction entitled *Psychosis: Tales of Madness*.

PIUS GONE hopscotches back and forth between the places willing to call him home: Tucson and Flagstaff, Arizona. While in transit, he tends to advocate for LGBTQ youth as an English teacher of three years, create robotic/vegetal installations with the Sound 1 collective and practice his jealousy-ridden cello. He will begin the MFA in Poetry program at the University of Arizona in August 2012.

D. GILSON is a teaching fellow at Chatham University. His chapbook, *Catch & Release*, won the 2011 Robin Becker Prize from Seven Kitchens

Press. His work has appeared in *Moon City Review, Plain Spoke, The Los Angeles Review* and elsewhere. [www.dgilson.com]

REBECCA LYNNE FULLAN is a writer of various stripes who teaches and studies English in the City University of New York system. She has also tutored students from the ages of five to 40 in more subjects than she has any knowledge of. She lives with her girlfriend, the playwright Charlotte Rahn-Lee, who listens to all her poems and a good number of other things she says besides. [www.rebeccalynnefullan.wordpress.com]

JIM ELLEDGE's *H*, a collection of prose poems, was published in 2012 from Lethe Press, and his biography of Henry Darger, *Throw-Away Boy*, is forthcoming from Overlook Press in 2013. His *A History of My Tattoo: A Poem* won the Lambda Literary Award and the Georgia Author of the Year award in poetry, both in 2006. His work has appeared in *Paris Review, Jubilat, Five Fingers Review, Denver Quarterly, North American Review, Amerika* and other journals. He directs the MA in Professional Writing Program at Kennesaw State University and lives in Atlanta.

MEG DAY is a three-time Pushcart-nominated poet, nationally awarded spoken word artist and veteran arts educator who is currently a PhD fellow in Poetry and Disability Poetics at the University of Utah. Meg hails from Oakland where she taught young poets to hold their own at the mic with YouthSpeaks and as a WritersCorps Teaching Artist in San Francisco. A 2010 Lambda Fellow, 2011 Hedgebrook Fellow and 2012 Squaw Valley Fellow, Meg completed her MFA at Mills College and now lives and writes in Salt Lake City. You can find her most recent work in forthcoming from the *Anthology of Trans and Genderqueer Poetry* (2012). [www.megday.com]

THERESA DAVIS is the mother of three and has been a classroom teacher for over twenty years. She reclaimed her love for poetry after the loss of her father. Since then, she has been a member of the Art Amok Slam Team and has been voted Best of Gay Atlanta in poetry and spoken word by *Creative Loafing, SOVO* and *Georgia Voice*. She won the title of Women of the World Slam Champion (2011), has been poet in residence as the McEver Chair of Georgia Tech University, was an Emerging Artist Grant Recipient and was honored by the City of Atlanta with a proclamation making May 22 *Theresa Davis Day*. Theresa uses her tongue for bounty. She's shiny and says stuff you wish you did.

PENELOPE DANE lives in Baton Rouge, Louisiana, with her partner and two cats. Winner of the William Jay Smith MFA Poetry award for her poem "Lesbian Potential," she has an MFA from Louisiana State University. Currently, she is working on her PhD and writing a novel about a ceramic artist. She rides a green scooter.

LOUIE CREW is an Alabama native and an emeritus professor at Rutgers. He lives in East Orange, New Jersey, with Ernest Clay, his husband of 38 years. Crew and Julie Penelope co-founded the LGBTQ caucus of the National Council of Teachers of English (1976). Crew edited the book *The Gay Academic* (1978). Editors have published 2,194 of Crew's poems and essays.

EC CRANDALL's poems and essays have been published in *PANK*, *Jupiter 88*, *The Anthology of Trans and Genderqueer Poetry*, *Gay Shame*, *Vexed by the Victorians* and *The Trans Literary Reader*. EC is co-author of the satirical erotic novel *Executive Privilege* and teaches in the University Writing Program at Columbia University.

MICHAEL G. CORNELIUS is an associate professor of English and the author/editor of numerous books.

CHARLOTTE CLUTTERBUCK belatedly jumped the fence at 58 and now lives with her girlfriend in Canberra. She writes poems and essays and teaches English Literature, Grammar, Academic Skills and Creative Writing. Charlotte is currently working on the Wheelbarrow Project, a series of right-brain exercises that aim to use risk, surprise, collaboration and delay to break down writers block and encourage flow.

JAMES CIHLAR is the author of the poetry books *Undoing* (Little Pear Press, 2008), *Rancho Nostalgia* (Dream Horse Press, 2013) and the chapbook *Metaphysical Bailout* (Pudding House Press, 2010). His writing appears in *American Poetry Review*, *Prairie Schooner*, *Lambda Literary Review*, *Smartish Pace*, *Mary* and *Forklift, Ohio*.

RENNY CHRISTOPHER is Associate Provost at California State University Channel Islands. Her memoir, *A Carpenter's Daughter: A Working-Class Woman in Higher Education* (Sense Publishers, 2009), addresses her experiences as the first in her family to attend college. Her poetry chapbook *My Name is Medea* won the New Spirit Press award in 1996; *Longing Fervently for Revolution* won the Slipstream Press competition in 1998; *Viet Nam and California* was published by Burning Cities Press in 1998. A print version of her performance piece "Middle-Class Drag" recently appeared in *Resilience: Queer Professors from the Working Class*, Kenneth Oldfield and Richard Greggory Johnson, editors.

JAMES BURFORD is a community development practitioner and educator living in the south island of Aotearoa-New Zealand. James has previously worked as a youth worker in Dunedin and as a coordinator for student services for queer/trans/takataapui students studying at Otago University. James is currently a doctoral student at the University of Auckland in the faculty of education. His recent work has focussed on doctoral students' emotional experiences of writing and the impacts of short gender/sexuality interventions on secondary school climates.

ELIZABETH BRADFIELD is the author of two collections of poetry: *Approaching Ice* and *Interpretive Work*. Her poems have appeared in *The Atlantic Monthly, Orion, The Believer* and *Poetry*, and she has been awarded the Audre Lorde Prize, a Stegner Fellowship from Stanford University and a scholarship to the Bread Loaf Writer's Conference, among other honors. The founder and editor-in-chief of Broadsided Press, she lives on Cape Cod and works as a teacher and naturalist. [www.broadsidedpress.org]

ELIZABETH BOSKEY is a queer woman and former professor of public health. She currently makes her living as a freelance writer, primarily writing about human sexuality. She is hard at work on her first book of poetry, *Personal Demons*. [www.elizabethboskey.com]

TOBY BIELAWSKI is a Bay Area writer and has published poetry in many journals and anthologies. Her chapbook, *Five Kinds of Fences*, won the New Word Order contest and was published in 2011 by Drafty Attic Press. She teaches and runs a poetry slam at Las Positas College and is currently Poet Laureate of Albany, California.

OLIVER BENDORF is an MFA candidate at the University of Wisconsin-Madison, where he taught creative writing for one year. His poems have appeared in *Ninth Letter, Anti-, PANK, The Journal* and elsewhere. He writes for *Original Plumbing* magazine and is at work on a manuscript of poems that investigates gender identity and language.

LIZ AHL is the author of the chapbooks *Luck* (Pecan Grove Press, 2010) and *A Thirst That's Partly Mine*, which won the 2008 Slapering Hol Press chapbook contest. Individual poems have appeared recently or are forthcoming in *Hayden's Ferry Review, Measure, North American Review* and *Iron Horse Literary Review*. She lives in New Hampshire.

ABOUT THE EDITOR

Megan Volpert lives in Atlanta, where she has taught high school English since 2006. She has a Master of Fine Arts in Creative Writing from Louisiana State University. Volpert is the author of four books: *Face Blindness* (BlazeVOX Books, 2007), *Domestic Transmission* (MetroMania Press, 2007), *The Desense of Nonfense* (BlazeVOX Books, 2009), and *Sonics in Warholia* (Sibling Rivalry Press, 2011). She is Co-Director of The Atlanta Queer Literary Festival, serves on the board of Poetry Atlanta, and has been in competition at the National Poetry Slam. You can find out more at www.meganvolpert.com.

ABOUT THE PRESS

Founded in 2010, Sibling Rivalry Press is an independent publishing house based in Alexander, Arkansas. Our mission is to publish work that disturbs and enraptures. We are proud to be the home to *Assaracus*, the world's only print journal of gay male poetry. Our titles have been honored by the American Library Association through inclusion on its annual "Over the Rainbow" list of recommended LGBT reading and by *Library Journal*, who named *Assaracus* as a best new magazine of 2011. While we champion our LGBTIQ authors and artists, we are an inclusive publishing house and welcome all authors, artists and readers regardless of sexual orientation or identity. For more information, visit our website at www.siblingrivalrypress.com.

If you enjoyed this anthology of poetry, you may also enjoy *Collective Brightness: LGBTIQ Poets on Faith, Religion and Spirituality* (edited by Kevin Simmonds). For more about *Collective Brightness*, visit our website.

CPSIA information can be obtained at www.ICGtesting.com
Printed in the USA
LVOW13s2016270913

354320LV00005B/279/P